ItsDeductible™

Turning Donations Into Dollars

Taxpayer Name_____

Taxpayer Social Security Number_____

NOTE: This workbook is copyrighted and can be used solely by one taxpayer and only for the tax year 2003. Any other use of this workbook is strictly prohibited by law.

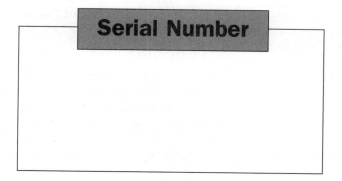

Serial Number

For more information, please write Publisher - ItsDeductible Workbook, Income Dynamics, 13911 Gold Circle, Omaha, NE 68144

ISBN 0-9703230-8-5

Distributed by Publishers Group West

Publisher's Note: Every effort was made, prior to publication of this workbook, to ensure that the information it contains was current, accurate and factual. The fair-market-values contained in the ItsDeductible workbook were made in accordance with current IRS regulations. Income Dynamics warrants the data included in this book to the extent detailed in the Dat*Assure*™ Warranty noted inside. This workbook is sold with the understanding that the publisher is not engaged in rendering legal, accounting or other professional service. Any specific tax questions should be directed at a professional tax preparer or accountant.

Money Back Guarantee: Income Dynamics guarantees that you will save at least $300 on your taxes this year by using this workbook or you can return the product to the Publisher for a refund of the full purchase price. In order to request a refund, return the workbook along with the completed Tax Preparation Worksheet (Page 116), proof of purchase and a brief explanation of your reason for return to Income Dynamics, Inc., Attn: Returns Department, 13911 Gold Circle, Suite 210, Omaha, NE 68144. For more details please visit www.ItsDeductible.com.

Table of Contents

Forward

Section 1 Turning Your Donations Into Dollars

How ItsDeductible Works.. 6

Getting Maximum Benefit from ItsDeductible... 7

Getting Started on Your Tax Savings 8

Section 2 Choosing A Qualified Organization

Who Qualifies as a "Charitable Organization"? 10

Qualified Organizations 10

Section 3 Valuing Donated Items

Value Categories 12

Other Factors that Affect Item Values 13

Designer Brands 13

Section 4 Other Charitable Donations

Out-of-Pocket Expenses 14

Fund-Raising Events 14

Monetary Donations.. 15

Property Donations... 15

Mileage Expenses... 16

Automobile Donations 17

Non-Deductible Donations 17

Section 5 Managing Your Donations

A Quick Review – Four Simple Steps.. 18

Some Rules to Know About 19

Federal Income Tax Brackets for 2003 20

IRS Tax Form 8283 21

DatAssure Warranty... 25

Warranty Registration Card 25

Section 6 Certified Market Valuations

Baby Supplies.. 27
Clothing, Boy's.. 29
Clothing, Girl's 33
Clothing, Infant's.. 37
Clothing, Men's 39
Clothing, Toddler's 44
Clothing, Women's 47
Designer Clothing, Men's 53
Designer Clothing, Women's 57
Electric Appliances, Large.. 62
Electric Appliances, Small.. 63
Electronics, Consumer 67
Entertainment 68
Exercise Equipment.. 71
Furniture 73
Games... 74
Garden Tools 77
Household Miscellaneous.. 78
Jewelry 80
Linens... 81
Pet Supplies 82
Sporting Goods 85
Tools 90
Toys... 92

Section 7 Valuation Worksheets

Custom Item Donations 94
Property Donations.. 100
Mileage Expense Tracking... 102
Monetary Donation Tracking.. 104
Out-of-Pocket Expense Tracking 108
Charity Information 112
Tax Preparation Worksheet... 116
Notes 117

Forward

Radio and TV great, Arthur Godfrey, said it so well… *"I'm proud to be paying taxes in the United States. The only thing is – I could be just as proud for half the money."*

Over the course of my two decades as a lawyer, author and tax accountant, I have counseled thousands of taxpayers on every kind of legal tax saving tip and technique. Experience tells me that cutting taxes in half may be unrealistic, but it always amazes me that some of the biggest breaks can be the easiest to overlook. That's why this book, ItsDeductible™, is so powerful.

The deduction for non-cash charitable giving is often referred to as "the most overlooked tax deduction in America." Over 20 million taxpayers donate goods to charity each year and grossly underestimate the value of those donated goods, often by as much as 80%! This simple deduction can easily save taxpayers hundreds of dollars in taxes.

Why do so many Americans miss the mark, you ask? The fault lies in two areas: a lack of proper tools for the taxpayer to use and the tax code itself. The IRS is charged with generating tax revenues within the boundaries of the tax code, but many times they will only give "guidelines", not hard and fast directions in interpreting the tax code. Non-cash donations fall into the category of guidelines…taxpayers determine what a fair-market-value is for a given donated item. More often than not, it's a guess. That's the beauty of ItsDeductible – all the guesswork has been eliminated.

Income Dynamics is the undisputed expert in fair-market valuations. They have the process down to a science. They ought to; they've been at it for 14 years. Their database of values has been developed from on-site surveys and sophisticated computer modeling based on MIT technology. This 2003 edition is the most comprehensive yet, including helpful tax tips, updated website addresses and their rock solid Dat*Assure*™ warranty.

In my best selling book, ***How to Pay Zero Taxes***, I describe many different legal tax strategies and techniques, including the deduction for non-cash charitable contributions. ItsDeductible will not only simplify the process it will maximize your tax deduction. If you itemize your deductions, and give household goods to charity, even one bag, you owe it to yourself to use this workbook. You may not cut your taxes in half, but you'll cut them by at least $300, ***guaranteed.*** Now, that's something to be proud of!

Jeff A. Schnepper
Financial, tax and legal advisor
Author, How to Pay Zero Taxes™

Section 1 Turning Your Donations Into Dollars

How ItsDeductible Works

An On-going Problem...Overpaying Your Taxes

Every year 20 million Americans give clothing, toys and other household items to charity but greatly underestimate the value of those donations on their taxes. As a result, taxpayers miss out on hundreds of dollars of tax savings, fully allowed by the IRS. You may be one of those taxpayers. The resulting problem–overpaying your taxes.

ItsDeductible is the solution. This revolutionary tax tool determines and assigns the actual fair-market-value to thousands of commonly donated items, allowing you to take advantage of your legal rights and significantly increase your tax deductions.

Our Legal Rights

IRS publications 526 and 561 both state that it is our legal right to deduct the "fair-market-value" of donated items. However, the IRS does not provide a guide to help taxpayers value their donations but rather suggests taxpayers compare their donated items to similar items found in thrift and consignment stores in order to get an indication of the fair-market-value. Because of the time and effort involved, most taxpayers choose not to do this and therefore miss one of the most significant tax deductions available today.

How We Determine Values

Using patent-pending Intelligent Indexing™ technology, combined with a nationwide network of manual data collection, ItsDeductible has organized and compiled this data into a powerful set of tools that accurately applies the fair-market-value to thousands of commonly donated items. Each item is given a specific value based on condition, age and market demand.

Since fair-market-values are constantly changing, the valuations within ItsDeductible are updated annually to provide users with current fair-market valuations. Taxpayers must use the most up-to-date information in order to comply with IRS guidelines.

TIP–Stay Current

Always use the most current information. A new ItsDeductible workbook or electronic record should be completed each year and filed with the corresponding year's tax information.

How Much Can You Save?

Without ItsDeductible

Donated to Charity

- dresser
- 3 bags of clothes
- lawn mower

Your Estimated Value $ 300

Tax Savings (Assumes 34% tax rate)   **$ 108**

With ItsDeductible

Donated Items	Number	Value	Total
Girl's Blouses and Shirts	12 - Fair	$ 5	$ 60
Girl's Casual Dresses	8 - Good	$ 15	$ 120
Men's Designer Silk Ties	8 - Good	$ 17	$ 136
Women's Designer Dress Winter Coat	2 - Fair	$ 60	$ 120
Women's Long Formal	2 - Good	$ 120	$ 240
Men's Denim Pants	5 - Good	$ 9	$ 45
Men's Two Piece Suits	2 - Good	$ 110	$ 220
Women's Dresses	4 - Fair	$ 20	$ 80
Men's Long Sleeve Shirts	6 - Fair	$ 8	$ 48
Women's Designer Pull Over Sweaters	5 - Good	$ 30	$ 150
Dresser	1 - Good	$ 169	$ 169
Lawn Mower	1 - Good	$ 162	$ 162

Actual Value Using ItsDeductible $ 1,550

Tax Savings (Assumes 34% tax rate)   **$ 522**

The exact amount of your savings will depend on your marginal tax rate. The marginal tax rate is the percentage of your income (over a base amount) that you pay in taxes.

Getting Maximum Benefit from ItsDeductible

To receive the maximum benefit from ItsDeductible, consider it to be your comprehensive donation guide and management tool. It has all the tools you need to accurately value every item you donate to charity and report it on your tax return. This workbook includes:

- Certified fair-market-values for over 2,000 commonly donated items
- Custom item donation forms for unique donations such as automobiles
- Information forms for each organization to which you donate
- Tax preparation worksheets to assist you or your accountant, which summarize all your donations

In addition, ItsDeductible also provides worksheets to track and deduct out-of-pocket expenses, mileage expenses and cash donations. These donations can add up to significant tax savings if they are organized and tracked properly. Keep this workbook handy throughout the year and use it whenever you make a donation to charity.

Why Not Have a Garage Sale?

Like most people, you've probably had a garage sale to recoup some of the money you've spent on your family's clothes and household goods. Garage sales, unfortunately, involve the expense of advertising, preparing signs and the time to mark, sort and price

each item. Add to that, sitting in the hot sun with strangers parading in and out of your garage. In addition, most items sell for only fifty-cents to a dollar. Donating your items to a qualified charity will generate tax savings for you while benefiting those less fortunate.

> ### TIP–Don't Wait for Your Refund!
>
> It's great to think of getting a larger tax refund next April, but you don't have to wait. Ask your employer for a new W-4 Withholding Form and simply increase the number of your exemptions. As a general guideline, if your donation total for the year approaches $2,700 claim one additional exemption on your W-4 form. This reduces the amount of tax withheld from your paycheck each pay period, providing you with tax savings throughout the entire year.

Getting Started on Your Tax Savings

Getting started is sometimes the hardest part of any task. However, knowing how much you can gain by cleaning out that cluttered closet or garage can be a great incentive. This workbook will take you step by step through the process of maximizing your charitable contributions. It's an easy task if you follow these simple steps:

Step 1 – Start by cleaning out one closet. Separate and place similar items into piles: shirts, pants, dresses, etc.

Step 2 – Choose the charity to which you want to donate your items. Section 2 of this workbook discusses qualified charitable organizations.

Step 3 – Use ItsDeductible to record and value the items separated into piles. The worksheets in Section 6 contain certified valuations on over 2,000 items. Section 3 of the workbook contains information regarding how to value items that are not shown in the worksheets.

> ### TIP–Snap a Photograph!
>
>
>
> It's always a good idea to have more documentation than less, if there's ever a question about a donation. In addition to the receipt the charity gives you, snap a photograph of the piles you make in Step 1 above. File the photo with the receipt and this workbook.

Step 4 – Place the items into boxes or bags and call the charity to pick them up or drop them off yourself. Be sure to request and save a receipt from the charity. The charity will not value the items but the receipt will serve as evidence that the items you listed in this workbook were donated.

Step 5 – Go to another closet or out to the garage and start back at Step 1. You'll be amazed at the potential tax savings waiting for you there.

TIP–Don't Forget to Record Your Mileage

Did you know you can legally deduct the travel costs associated with delivering your items to the charity? The mileage deduction is 14 cents per mile. You can also include any parking and toll fees. Section 4 details other Charitable Donations that can add up to additional tax savings each year.

Section 2 Choosing a Qualified Organization

Who Qualifies as a "Charitable Organization"?

You can deduct charitable contributions only if they are made to or for the use of a "qualified charitable organization." To qualify, an organization must be a corporation, community chest, fund or foundations organized and operated exclusively for charitable purposes as described in IRS Section 501(c)(3). The earnings of the organization may not accumulate for the benefit of any private shareholder or individual. In addition, a charitable organization may not attempt to influence legislation as a substantial part of its activities and it may not participate at all in campaign activities for or against political candidates.

IRS Publication 78 is a cumulative list of the organizations to which contributions are deductible. The list can be found by visiting the ItsDeductible website, **www.ItsDeductible.com**. Simply click on the direct link to this information under "Tax Resources – IRS Forms and Docs". The list identifies each type of charitable organization and is updated annually. Supplements may also be obtained on a subscription basis from the Superintendent of Documents, Government Printing Office, Washington, D.C. 20402

Qualified Organizations

A contribution is deductible if it is given to or for the use of the following qualified organizations:
1) A State, a U.S. possession, or political subdivision, of the United States, or the District of Columbia, if made exclusively for public purposes.
2) A community chest, corporation, trust fund, or foundation, organized or created in the United States or its possessions and organized and operated exclusively for charitable, religious, educational, scientific, or literary purposes, or for the prevention of cruelty to children or animals.
3) A church, synagogue, or other religious organization.
4) A war veterans' organization, its post, auxiliaries, trusts or foundations organized in the United States or its possessions.
5) A civil defense organization created under Federal, State, or local law.
6) A domestic fraternal society, operating under the lodge system, but only if the contribution is to be used exclusively for charitable, religious, educational, scientific, or literary purposes, or for the prevention of cruelty to children or animals.
7) A nonprofit cemetery company if the funds are irrevocably dedicated to the perpetual care of the cemetery as a whole and not a particular lot or mausoleum crypt.
8) Indian tribal governments, which are treated as states for purposes of charitable contributions.

Some of the 501(c)(3) organizations that qualify, based on the above definitions include:
- Amvets
- The Boys of America
- Girl Scouts of the USA
- Goodwill Industries International
- Churches/Synagogues
- American Council of the Blind
- Disabled American Veterans
- Federal, State & Local Governments
- Public Parks and Recreation
- American Red Cross
- The Salvation Army
- American Society for Deaf Children
- Tax-exempt educational institutions
- Tax-exempt hospitals

If you have questions about an organization's tax status, contact the organization directly and ask if they qualify for tax-exempt status.

TIP–Individuals Aren't Allowed!

Contributions to an individual or individuals cannot be taken as a deduction. The IRS has ruled that there is no assurance that the contribution will actually make its way to the charity. This includes contributions to individual ministers. Donate, instead, to the minister's religious organization or church.

Section 3 Valuing Donated Items

To accurately determine your tax deduction, you will need to assign a value to the items you donate. According to the Internal Revenue Service, you can deduct the fair-market-value of clothing, toys, household goods, used furniture, shoes, books, or any item you donate to a qualified charity. IRS Publication 561 states that the fair-market-value is determined as, "the price that would be agreed upon between a willing buyer and a willing seller, with neither being required to act, and both having reasonable knowledge of the relevant facts."

ItsDeductible has established the fair-market-values for you. Using patent-pending Intelligent Indexing™ technology, combined with a nationwide network of manual data collections, ItsDeductible has determined and assigned values to thousands of commonly donated items, all in accordance with IRS guidelines. ItsDeductible establishes the value based upon the condition of the item: good, fair or poor.

Value Categories

The value of an item is affected by the condition of the item. For example, a suit worn only a few times with no apparent wear would be valued higher than one showing noticeable wear.

The Certified Market Valuation section, beginning on page 25, provides you with worksheets to indicate the quantity and condition of each item you donate. The charity will not provide item values for you. Using ItsDeductible, however, makes this process quick and easy.

As a result of research and analysis, ItsDeductible provides values in three categories, **"High," "Medium"** or **"Low."** These values are defined as:

- **HIGH VALUE**
  An item in good condition, showing no noticeable wear or defects.

- **MEDIUM VALUE**
  An item in fair condition, showing slight wear or defects.

- **LOW VALUE**
  An item in poor condition, showing appreciable wear or defects.

Other Factors That Affect Item Values

Additional factors can affect the value of your donated items. According to IRS Publication 561, these factors include desirability, use and scarcity. These same factors have been taken into account in the values provided within ItsDeductible and must be considered when you are assigning values to items not listed by ItsDeductible (Custom Items). For more information about Custom Items, see page 94.

NOTE: ItsDeductible serves as a guideline to assist you in establishing the value of your donated items. The IRS expects taxpayers to make a "good faith effort" when determining the value of donated items. The taxpayer is ultimately responsible for assigning the value category and must be able to substantiate their decision.

Designer Brands

Designer and/or upscale name-brand apparel and accessories carry a higher fair-market-value due to the quality and craftsmanship. Designer brand listings begin on page 53 of this workbook.

Examples of Designer and Name-brand Clothing:

- Bill Blass
- Hugo Boss
- Giorgio Armani
- Coach
- Liz Claiborne
- Jones New York
- Chaus

- Ralph Lauren
- Polo
- Guess
- Tommy Hilfiger
- Calvin Klein
- Dior
- Yves St. Laurent

- DKNY
- Nautica
- Perry Ellis
- Johnston & Murphy
- Nine West
- Ann Taylor

TIP—I can't find my item in the workbook!

The ItsDeductible workbook contains over 2,000 commonly donated items, but you may have an item that is not listed. If that's the case, visit StrongNumbers.com or Ebay.com to find the fair-market-values of the unique items you want to donate.

ItsDeductible™
Turning Donations Into Dollars

Section 4 Other Charitable Donations

Donations can take many different forms. For example, if you perform volunteer work for a charity or church and spend your own money or use your own vehicle, you can deduct your actual expenses. However, you cannot deduct the value of your services, your knowledge or your time.   Other forms of donations are listed below.

Out-of-Pocket Expenses

Out-of-pocket donations are defined as expenses incurred while performing volunteer charitable work, or as a function of participation in or with a tax-exempt organization.

Examples include:
- Buying doughnuts for a church youth group
- Purchasing movie tickets for a Boy Scouts troop outing
- Buying an airline ticket for travel on a mission trip
- Purchasing Sunday School materials or literature
- Taking someone to lunch to discuss fund-raising

Fund-raising events may also be considered an out-of-pocket donation, however, certain restrictions apply, as noted below.

> **TIP–Teachers Get a Special Break!**
>
> For tax years 2002 and 2003, K-12 educators receive a special deduction called the Educator Deduction. Teachers can deduct up to $250 off their income if they spend out-of-pocket money for classroom supplies. Use the Out-Of-Pocket Expenses section to stay within IRS reporting guidelines.   Keep a record of the **date**, **amount** and **purpose** of each expense. Be watching for 2004 – this deduction is projected to increase to $400.

Fund-Raising Events

Have you ever wondered if you could deduct the cost of a ticket to a charity event, or the cost of something you bought at a charity auction or bazaar? Parts of those costs are deductible if the price you paid is more than the benefit you received.

Examples:
- If you paid $40 for a ticket to attend a charity auction, and the price includes a meal valued at $15, then you can deduct the difference of $25 as a charitable donation.
- If you paid $100 for an item at a charity auction and the item had a fair-market-value of $60, then you can deduct the remaining $40.
- If you make a contribution of more than $75 to a qualified organization that is partly for goods or services you receive, the organization must give you a written statement.

Charities are now required to state the deductible amount of your contribution on the face of the ticket. Be sure to retain the ticket for your records. In some instances, you may be able to deduct 100% of the cost. Check our website at **www.ItsDeductible.com** and click **"Deduction Information"** for more information.

Monetary Donations

Monetary Donations are donations made to a charitable organization in the form of cash, check, credit card or debit card.

Whether you place $20 in a church offering or pledge $100 to the American Cancer Association, the transaction can be logged and managed in the Monetary Donations section (page 104) of ItsDeductible. The Monetary Donations section allows for convenient tracking of monthly or annual donations. Tracking includes the payment method, consisting of the specific credit card or check number used for your donation.

TIP–Instead of Cash, Give Stock

If you have owned shares of a stock for more than one year and the stock has appreciated in value, donate some of those shares instead of cash. You get to deduct the fair-market-value of the stock and avoid paying capital gains taxes as well!

Property Donations

A property donation is defined as a donation of stocks, bonds, or mutual funds to a qualified organization. Depending on the value of the property and the time you donate it, this donation will be either an Ordinary Income Property Donation or a Capital Gain Property Donation.

Ordinary Income Property Donations

An Ordinary Income Property Donation means that, at the time you donated the property, the stocks, bonds, or mutual funds donated were owned by you for less than a twelve month period of time. The IRS considers that a short term capital gain or simply, ordinary income. For example, you bought 100 shares of XYZ stock at $10 per share, but just eight months later you donated that stock to your church when the value of this stock was at $15 per share. This would be an Ordinary Income Donation, so you will only be able to deduct from your taxes the original basis (the original $1,000) of the property, rather than its full fair-market-value.

Capital Gain Property Donations

The second type of property donation is a Capital Gain Property donation. If you have owned a stock, bond or mutual fund for more than twelve months, at the time you make the donation, it is considered a capital gain donation. The IRS views this as a Long Term Capital Gain. For example, you bought the same 100 shares of XYZ stock at $10 per share, and fourteen months later you donated them to your church when the per share price was $15. In this case, since you have had the stock for greater than 12 months, you can deduct the entire fair-market-value of the stock (which is now $1,500) on your tax return.

There are some limitations on Property Donations if your contributions exceed 20% of your Adjusted Gross Income. The amount of your deduction may be limited to either 20%, 30% or 50% of your adjusted gross income, depending on the type of property you give and the type of charity. For more detailed information, check out IRS Publication 526 on Charitable Contributions. You can find it at **http://www.ItsDeductible.com/ prodsupport/publications.html**.

TIP—When Not to Donate

There is one instance in which you should consider not donating your property to a qualified organization. This is the case where the fair-market-value of your property has gone down in value since the time you originally purchased it. In this case, you are better off selling the property at a loss, deducting the loss on your taxes, and then donating the proceeds to the qualified organization.

Mileage Expenses

Travel costs are deductible as a charitable donation when they are not reimbursed by the charity. The current IRS mileage deduction is 14 cents per mile. Toll and parking fees can be deducted in addition to the 14-cent mileage deduction.

Some charitable activities that could result in tax deductions for using your vehicle are:
- Voluntary administrative duties at a local church
- Delivery of clothing donations to a charity
- Travel related to Vacation Bible School
- Delivery of Meals on Wheels
- Travel related to coaching sports teams sponsored by tax-exempt organizations (churches, city recreation departments, youth sports, etc.)
- Religious or school-related activities, such as youth field trips or driving children to Scout or church camp

TIP—Vacations Are Not Allowed!

Mileage deductions can add up, but be careful. No deduction is allowed if there is any significant personal pleasure, vacation or recreation involved in the travel for charity.

Automobile Donations

The IRS released a Service Center Advice memorandum that discusses the valuation method, which should be used in valuing automobiles given to a charitable organization. The memo indicates the fair-market-value of the vehicle is the amount that a willing buyer would pay a willing seller, when each has relevant knowledge of the facts. The fair-market-value can be established by using car guidebooks such as Kelly Blue Book or the National Automobile Dealer's Association (NADA) Used Car Guide. For Internet users, you can visit our website at **www.ItsDeductible.com** and link to the Kelly Blue Book website for used car values.

Non-deductible Donations

Some charity-related transactions are not deductible:
* Purchasing but not using tickets to a charitable event. This is because you have purchased a privilege, whether or not you used it.
* Paying fair-market-value for an item at a charity auction. The price you paid must exceed the item's value in order for the difference to be deductible.
* Blood donations to the American Red Cross or blood banks (mileage is deductible).
* Payment to a college or university where the tax donor receives a right to buy seating at an athletic event is 80% deductible as a contribution. No amount paid for the tickets themselves is deductible.
* Buying tickets for charity raffles, lotteries, bingo or similar drawings for valuable prizes is not deductible whether you win a prize or not.
* The value of income lost while you work as an unpaid volunteer for a qualified organization.

TIP–Donate Those Dusty Old Textbooks

If you have old college textbooks or professional books that are taking up space, donate them to your local library. You can take a deduction even if the books were given to you as a gift.

ItsDeductible™
Turning Donations Into Dollars

Section 5 Managing Your Donations

Managing your donations is what ItsDeductible is all about – an easy and efficient method for organizing and valuing all charitable donations. Listed below is a short review of the steps to using ItsDeductible. It's also helpful to be aware of some of the deduction rules and the current Federal Tax brackets. These are discussed at the end of this section.

A Quick Review...Four Simple Steps

1. Locate your donated item in the Certified Market Valuations section. Indicate the quantity and value category for the items donated and then tally your extended total.
2. Record each donation, along with the charity name, address, the date and total value donated, on the chart provided on page 112.
3. Arrange your items on the floor, sofa or bed and take a snapshot or video. While this is not required, it will substantiate your contribution if questions ever arise. Keep the visual record with your personal tax records. Do not include them with your tax return. (If you have already donated your goods and did not take a photo, simply skip this step.)
4. When making your donation, obtain a SIGNED, DATED receipt for your donations. Your donation must be made by December 31, 2003 in order to claim this donation on your 2003 tax return.

You are not required to have a receipt where it is impractical to get one (for example, if you leave property at a charity's unattended drop site). Just document this fact in the back of the workbook.

The Omnibus Budget Reconciliation Act of 1993 states that a taxpayer must substantiate any contribution of $250 or more at the time of the donation with a written acknowledgment from the organization, unless the organization files a statement with the IRS that contains the required information. Most, however, do not file this information, so you need to obtain a signed dated receipt of your donation.

TIP–Some Simple Suggestions
- Use "Hash" marks when you have more than one item in a particular category.
- Record multiple donations throughout the year by designating each donation with a different color of ink.

Rules Regarding Charitable Donations

Like all tax matters, there are a few rules regarding charitable donations:

If your donation of clothing and household goods is more than $500, IRS Form 8283 must be filed with your tax return. All information needed to complete Form 8283 is included in this workbook.

An outside appraisal is required if the total value of a donated item or group of similar items exceeds $5,000. Similar items of property are items of the same generic category or type, such as stamp collections, coin collections, lithographs, paintings, books, non-publicly traded stock, land or buildings.

> Example: You claimed a deduction of $2,100 for clothing and $6,000 for a collection of books. Report the clothing in Section A of Form 8283 and the books (a group of similar items, which requires an appraisal) in Section B of Form 8283.

Most donated clothing and household items will not be worth more than what you paid for them. If you have owned an item for less than one year, the most you can deduct is the amount you paid for it. If you owned an item for more than one year, you can deduct the current fair-market-value for that item, even if the fair-market-value is more than the amount you paid.

There are instances when your property may have increased in value. For detailed information, refer to IRS Publication 561, "Determining the Value of Donated Property."

Examples of determining the actual value of donated items:

> Example 1: A pair of men's hiking books in good condition (no noticeable wear) is worth $20 as a deduction. However, if you only paid $16 for those boots six months ago, the most you can deduct is $16.

> Example 2: If you have a six-month-old name brand coffee maker but it's in poor condition, then you must select the low-value category and take only the $5 deduction.

> Example 3: If you buy a designer leather purse in good condition for $20 at a garage sale and fifteen months later, you donate this purse to charity in fair condition, then you can deduct $38, the fair-market-value for this item, in accordance with IRS guidelines.

ItsDeductible™
Turning Donations Into Dollars

Federal Income Tax Brackets For 2003

Tax Rate	Married	Single
10%	$0 – $14,000	$0 – $7000
15%	$14,001 – $56,800	$7001 – $28,400
25%	$56,801 – $114,650	$28,401 – $68,800
28%	$114,651 – $174,700	$68,801 – $143,500
33%	$174,701 – $311,950	$143,501 – $311,950
35%	$311,951 and above	$311,951 and above

If you are married and your taxable income is from $56,801 to $114,650, you are in the 25 percent tax bracket and every $100 in deductions saves you $25 in federal taxes. ($100.00 x 25% = $25.00)

You save even more if you pay state income taxes. The marginal tax rate in many states averages 6% or an additional $6 saved for every $100 in donations. This means a total savings of $31 for every $100 worth of donations.

Example: $25.00 Federal Tax Savings
         + $6.00 State Tax Savings
              $31.00 Total Tax Savings

To determine your state tax rate, visit your state's tax website. You can reach it easily through the ItsDeductible website at: **http://www.ItsDeductible.com/html/help_statetax.shtml**

IRS Tax Form 8283

You must complete the IRS Tax Form 8283 when the value of your donated items exceeds $500.

To print Tax Form 8283, visit our website at **www.ItsDeductible.com** and click on "IRS Forms and Docs," or visit the IRS website directly.

Sample Tax Form 8283:

Form **8283** (Rev. October 1998) Department of the Treasury Internal Revenue Service	**Noncash Charitable Contributions** ▶ Attach to your tax return if you claimed a total deduction of over $500 for all contributed property. ▶ See separate instructions.	OMB No. 1545-0908 Attachment Sequence No. **55**

Name(s) shown on your income tax return | Identifying number

Note: *Figure the amount of your contribution deduction before completing this form. See your tax return instructions.*

Section A– List in this section **only** items (or groups of similar items) for which you claimed a deduction of $5,000 or less. Also, list certain publicly traded securities even if the deduction is over $5,000 (see instructions).

Part I   **Information on Donated Property–** If you need more space, attach a statement.

1	(a) Name and address of the donee organization	(b) Description of donated property
A		
B		
C		
D		
E		

Note: *If the amount you claimed as a deduction for an item is $500 or less, you do not have to complete columns (d), (e), and (f).*

	(c) Date of the contribution	(d) Date acquired by donor (mo., yr.)	(e) How acquired by donor	(f) Donor's cost or adjusted basis	(g) Fair market value	(h) Method used to determine the fair market value
A						
B						
C						
D						
E						

Part II   **Other Information–** Complete line 2 if you gave less than an entire interest in property listed in Part I. Complete line 3 if conditions were attached to a contribution listed in Part I.

2 If, during the year, you contributed less than the entire interest in the property, complete lines a–e.

a Enter the letter from Part I that identifies the property ▶ _____. If Part II applies to more than one property, attach a separate statement.

b Total amount claimed as a deduction for the property listed in Part I: **(1)** For this tax year   ▶ _____ .   **(2)** For any prior tax years   ▶ _____ .

c Name and address of each organization to which any such contribution was made in a prior year (complete only if different from the donee organization above):

Name of charitable organization (donee)

Address (number, street, and room or suite no.)

City or town, state, and ZIP code

d For tangible property, enter the place where the property is located or kept ▶ _____

e Name of any person, other than the donee organization, having actual possession of the property ▶ _____

3 If conditions were attached to any contribution listed in Part I, answer questions a – c and attach the required statement (see instructions).

		Yes	No
a	Is there a restriction, either temporary or permanent, on the donee's right to use or dispose of the donated property?		
b	Did you give to anyone (other than the donee organization or another organization participating with the donee organization in cooperative fundraising) the right to the income from the donated property or to the possession of the property, including the right to vote donated securities, to acquire the property by purchase or otherwise, or to designate the person having such income, possession, or right to acquire?		
c	Is there a restriction limiting the donated property for a particular use?		

For Paperwork Reduction Act Notice, see page 4 of separate instructions.   Cat. No. 62299J   Form **8283** (Rev. 10-98)

Page 2 (partial overlay)

Identifying number

...ar items) for which you claimed a ...contributions of certain publicly

the **Note** in Part I below. ...nd/or appraiser.

...lry   ☐ Stamp Collections   ☐ Other ...ative arts, textiles, carpets, silver, rare

...the signed appraisal. See instructions.

...nary of the overall   **(c)** Appraised fair market value

See instructions

...claimed as a   **(i)** Average trading price ...duction   of securities

...e that the appraisal identifies as ...ructions.

...n appraised value of not more than $500

Date ▶

...property, employed by, or related to any ...if regularly used by the donor, donee, or

...is; and that because of my qualifications ...fy that the appraisal fees were not based ...overstatement of the property value as ...section 6701(a) (aiding and abetting the ...y by the Director of Practice.

...ate of appraisal ▶

Identifying number

...tion.

...)(c) and that it received the donated

...s of the property described in Section ..., Donee Information Return, with the ...nt with the claimed fair market value.

Does the organization intend to use the property for an unrelated use? . . . . ▶ ☐ Yes   ☐ No

Name of charitable organization (donee)	Employer identification number
Address (number, street, and room or suite no.)	City or town, state, and ZIP code
Authorized signature	Title	Date

ItsDeductible™ For Your Computer

Keep Saving Tax Dollars!

Every year the ItsDeductible fair-market-value database is updated and over 70% of it changes. Always be sure that you are using the most current information available. This workbook is for the 2003 tax year. Order your 2004 copy today, so you can maximize your tax savings year after year.

Try ItsDeductible Software!

The software version of ItsDeductible offers many automated features such as item search capability that allows you to quickly and easily value your item donations. The software also provides you with a running total of your deductions

and tax savings, as well as many helpful reports, worksheets and Internet links. It even completes IRS Form 8283 automatically for you!

Try it yourself for only $19.95!

Place your order TODAY for ItsDeductible workbook or software. Go to www.ItsDeductible.com or call 800-976-5358.

ItsDeductible™
Turning Donations Into Dollars

Your Dat*Assure*™ Warranty!

The Dat*Assure* Warranty will take away any worries related to an IRS inquiry as it provides the following security:

- In the unlikely event that the IRS questions the values assigned to your donations, Income Dynamics, the maker of ItsDeductible, will provide the IRS with direct documentation supporting the fair-market-values provided by ItsDeductible.

- If you receive a fine or penalty from the IRS that is associated with your donation and the fair-market-values assigned to your donations, we will pay those fines and penalties for you, up to $5,000.

This gives you peace-of-mind, knowing you can use ItsDeductible with confidence!

Dat*Assure* Warranty

Income Dynamics hereby warrants that the fair-market-values contained in the ItsDeductible product were made in accordance with current IRS regulations. Income Dynamics assumes responsibility for any interest and penalties imposed by the IRS in the event any fair-market-value assigned to your donation is challenged, and is proven to have been improperly determined by ItsDeductible. You must have proof of your donation (e.g. receipt, etc.) that details what goods were donated, the condition of such goods, the date and location of the contribution, and the name of the donee. If any assigned fair-market-value has been altered, misstated, or miscalculated in any way by any means not associated with the functionality of ItsDeductible, this warranty shall be null and void.

Further, for this warranty to be effective, Income Dynamics must be notified immediately upon receipt of notice of any challenge of any fair-market-valuation calculated by ItsDeductible, and given full opportunity to participate in defending the same. This notification can be given by immediately writing to Income Dynamics, Inc. Attn: ItsDeductible Warranty Claim, 13911 Gold Circle, Suite 210, Omaha, NE 68144-2376. You should include within this notification a copy of the IRS notice and evidence of payment, if any, of the particular penalty and/or interest. Our warranty extends only to the registered ItsDeductible product owner. Any willful disregard for the copyright protection afforded ItsDeductible, by reproducing or copying in any way will invalidate this warranty. This warranty only applies to the tax year in which you purchase and use ItsDeductible. This warranty gives you specific legal rights, and you may also have other legal rights, which vary from State to State.

Section 6 Certified Market Valuations

Baby Supplies

Description	High* Good Condition	Average* Fair Condition	Low* Poor Condition	Total
Baby Monitors				
Name Brand	$23.00	$16.00	$3.00	
Other	$16.00	$11.00	$2.00	
Car Seats				
Name Brand	$64.00	$45.00	$10.00	
Other	$41.00	$29.00	$6.00	
Miscellaneous				
Bassinets	$61.00	$39.00	$15.00	
Bibs	$2.00	$1.00	$1.00	
Booster Seat	$11.00	$8.00	$3.00	
Bottle Dryers	$1.50	$1.00	$0.50	
Bottle Sets	$3.00	$2.00	$1.00	
Bottle Warmer	$10.00	$6.00	$3.00	
Bumper Pads	$12.00	$7.00	$3.00	
Carrier	$24.00	$14.00	$6.00	
Changing Pad	$4.00	$2.00	$1.00	
Changing Table	$60.00	$48.00	$15.00	
Crib	$192.00	$136.00	$48.00	
Diaper Bag	$14.00	$7.00	$3.00	
Dolls	$17.00	$6.00	$3.00	
High Chair	$25.00	$18.00	$6.00	
Johnny Jump-Up	$23.00	$18.00	$6.00	
Play Mats	$9.00	$5.00	$2.00	
Playpen	$43.00	$36.00	$11.00	
Potty Chair	$10.00	$7.00	$3.00	
Saucer	$21.00	$12.00	$5.00	

*See pages 12 & 13 for important information about properly valuing your donated items.

Baby Supplies

Description	High* Good Condition	Average* Fair Condition	Low* Poor Condition	Total
Scooter	$12.00	$8.00	$3.00	
Sling	$14.00	$11.00	$4.00	
Swing	$45.00	$35.00	$11.00	
Tub	$6.00	$4.00	$2.00	
Walker	$32.00	$23.00	$8.00	
Safety Gates				
Name Brand	$41.00	$28.00	$6.00	
Other	$32.00	$22.00	$5.00	
Strollers				
Name Brand	$110.00	$77.00	$16.00	
Other	$75.00	$52.00	$11.00	
TOTAL BABY SUPPLIES			$	

*See pages 12 & 13 for important information about properly valuing your donated items.

Clothing, Boy's

Description	High* Good Condition	Average* Fair Condition	Low* Poor Condition	Total
Accessories				
Belts				
Dress Leather	_____$6.00	_____$3.00	_____$1.00	_____
Other	_____$3.00	_____$2.00	_____$1.00	_____
Caps				
Baseball	_____$5.00	_____$3.00	_____$1.00	_____
Stocking	_____$3.00	_____$2.00	_____$1.00	_____
Sun Visor	_____$3.00	_____$2.00	_____$1.00	_____
Scarves				
Winter	_____$3.00	_____$2.50	_____$1.00	_____
Suspenders				
Button Clip-On	_____$4.00	_____$3.00	_____$1.00	_____
Ties	_____$4.00	_____$3.00	_____$1.00	_____
Exercise				
Jackets				
Fleece Insulated w/Hood	_____$11.00	_____$6.00	_____$3.00	_____
Fleece w/Hood	_____$10.00	_____$8.00	_____$3.00	_____
Pants				
Fleece	_____$5.00	_____$4.00	_____$1.00	_____
Nylon	_____$8.00	_____$6.00	_____$2.00	_____
Shirts				
Fleece Long-Sleeve	_____$7.00	_____$5.00	_____$2.00	_____
Fleece Short-Sleeve	_____$8.00	_____$6.00	_____$2.00	_____
Shorts				
Fleece	_____$6.00	_____$4.00	_____$1.00	_____
Nylon	_____$8.00	_____$5.00	_____$2.00	_____
Suits (Matching Pants and Top)				
Fleece	_____$7.00	_____$5.00	_____$2.00	_____
Nylon	_____$11.00	_____$7.00	_____$3.00	_____

See pages 12 & 13 for important information about properly valuing your donated items.

ItsDeductible™
Turning Donations Into Dollars

Clothing, Boy's

Description	High* Good Condition	Average* Fair Condition	Low* Poor Condition	Total
Outerwear				
Casual Jackets				
Cloth	_____ $9.00	_____ $7.00	_____ $2.00	_____
Denim	_____ $11.00	_____ $8.00	_____ $3.00	_____
Casual Winter Coats				
Ski	_____ $20.00	_____ $13.00	_____ $5.00	_____
Dress Winter Coats				
All Weather	_____ $38.00	_____ $23.00	_____ $10.00	_____
Mittens and Gloves	_____ $2.00	_____ $1.50	_____ $1.00	_____
Ski Pants	_____ $7.00	_____ $5.00	_____ $2.00	_____
Vests				
Winter	_____ $8.00	_____ $6.00	_____ $2.00	_____
Shirts				
Casual				
Flannel Long-Sleeve	_____ $8.00	_____ $5.00	_____ $2.00	_____
Long-Sleeve	_____ $7.00	_____ $5.50	_____ $2.00	_____
Short-Sleeve	_____ $7.50	_____ $5.00	_____ $2.00	_____
Turtleneck	_____ $5.00	_____ $4.00	_____ $1.00	_____
Dress				
Long-Sleeve	_____ $8.50	_____ $6.00	_____ $2.00	_____
Short-Sleeve	_____ $8.00	_____ $6.00	_____ $2.00	_____
Sport				
Pullover Long-Sleeve	_____ $5.00	_____ $4.00	_____ $1.00	_____
Pullover Short-Sleeve	_____ $7.00	_____ $5.00	_____ $2.00	_____
Shoes and Boots				
Boots, Snow	_____ $9.00	_____ $6.00	_____ $2.00	_____
Casual				
Boots Western	_____ $14.00	_____ $9.00	_____ $4.00	_____
Shoe Slip-On	_____ $8.00	_____ $6.00	_____ $2.00	_____
Shoe w/Laces	_____ $10.00	_____ $7.00	_____ $3.00	_____

See pages 12 & 13 for important information about properly valuing your donated items.

Clothing, Boy's

Description	High* Good Condition	Average* Fair Condition	Low* Poor Condition	Total
Dress				
Shoe Leather Slip-On	_____ $8.00	_____ $6.00	_____ $2.00	_____
Shoe Leather w/Laces	_____ $10.00	_____ $7.00	_____ $3.00	_____
Slippers	_____ $4.00	_____ $3.00	_____ $1.00	_____
Sport				
Sneaker Cloth	_____ $8.00	_____ $6.00	_____ $2.00	_____
Sneaker Leather	_____ $11.00	_____ $7.00	_____ $3.00	_____
Slacks and Pants				
Casual				
Corduroy	_____ $11.00	_____ $7.00	_____ $3.00	_____
Denim	_____ $10.00	_____ $7.00	_____ $2.00	_____
Other	_____ $9.00	_____ $6.00	_____ $2.00	_____
Dress	_____ $13.00	_____ $9.00	_____ $3.00	_____
Sleepwear				
Pajamas				
Set (Pants and Shirt)	_____ $7.00	_____ $4.00	_____ $2.00	_____
Robe	_____ $7.00	_____ $6.00	_____ $2.00	_____
Suits				
Casual				
Sport Coat	_____ $16.00	_____ $10.00	_____ $4.00	_____
Dress				
Coat	_____ $19.00	_____ $14.00	_____ $5.00	_____
Slacks	_____ $12.00	_____ $9.00	_____ $3.00	_____
Two-Piece	_____ $42.00	_____ $28.00	_____ $10.00	_____
Summerwear				
Shirts				
T-Shirt	_____ $6.00	_____ $4.00	_____ $2.00	_____
Tank	_____ $8.00	_____ $5.00	_____ $2.00	_____
Shorts				
Denim	_____ $7.00	_____ $5.00	_____ $2.00	_____
Other	_____ $6.00	_____ $5.00	_____ $2.00	_____
Swimwear	_____ $6.00	_____ $4.00	_____ $1.00	_____

See pages 12 & 13 for important information about properly valuing your donated items.

Clothing, Boy's

Description	High* Good Condition	Average* Fair Condition	Low* Poor Condition	Total
Sweaters				
Casual				
Cardigan	_____ $10.00	_____ $7.00	_____ $2.00	_____
Pullover Long-Sleeve	_____ $8.00	_____ $6.00	_____ $2.00	_____
V-Neck	_____ $9.00	_____ $5.00	_____ $2.00	_____
Vest	_____ $11.00	_____ $6.00	_____ $3.00	_____
Dress				
Cardigan	_____ $5.00	_____ $3.00	_____ $1.00	_____
Pullover Long-Sleeve	_____ $6.00	_____ $4.00	_____ $1.00	_____
V-Neck	_____ $5.00	_____ $3.00	_____ $1.00	_____
Vest	_____ $9.00	_____ $5.00	_____ $2.00	_____
Undergarments				
Pants				
Insulated	_____ $5.00	_____ $3.00	_____ $1.00	_____
Shirts				
Long-Sleeve Insulated	_____ $3.00	_____ $2.00	_____ $1.00	_____
T-Shirt	_____ $2.00	_____ $1.00	_____ $0.50	_____
Socks (Pair)				
Dress	_____ $2.00	_____ $1.00	_____ $0.50	_____
Other	_____ $2.00	_____ $1.00	_____ $0.50	_____
TOTAL CLOTHING, BOY'S				$

See pages 12 & 13 for important information about properly valuing your donated items.

Clothing, Girl's

Description	High* Good Condition	Average* Fair Condition	Low* Poor Condition	Total
Accessories				
Belts				
Leather	_____ $5.00	_____ $4.00	_____ $1.00	_____
Other	_____ $3.00	_____ $2.00	_____ $1.00	_____
Caps				
Biking	_____ $6.00	_____ $3.00	_____ $1.00	_____
Stocking	_____ $2.50	_____ $1.50	_____ $1.00	_____
Hats				
Dress	_____ $6.00	_____ $3.00	_____ $1.00	_____
Summer	_____ $5.00	_____ $4.00	_____ $1.00	_____
Purses	_____ $4.00	_____ $3.00	_____ $1.00	_____
Scarves	_____ $2.50	_____ $2.00	_____ $1.00	_____
Blouses and Shirts				
Casual				
Long-Sleeve	_____ $5.00	_____ $4.00	_____ $1.00	_____
Short-Sleeve	_____ $5.00	_____ $3.00	_____ $1.00	_____
Turtleneck	_____ $5.00	_____ $3.00	_____ $1.00	_____
Dress				
Long-Sleeve	_____ $6.50	_____ $5.00	_____ $2.00	_____
Short-Sleeve	_____ $6.00	_____ $5.00	_____ $2.00	_____
Dresses				
Casual	_____ $8.00	_____ $6.00	_____ $2.00	_____
Dress	_____ $16.00	_____ $10.00	_____ $4.00	_____
Summer	_____ $10.00	_____ $6.00	_____ $3.00	_____
Exercise				
Jackets				
Fleece Insulated w/Hood	_____ $11.00	_____ $8.00	_____ $3.00	_____
Fleece w/Hood	_____ $9.00	_____ $7.00	_____ $2.00	_____
Leotards	_____ $7.00	_____ $6.00	_____ $2.00	_____

See pages 12 & 13 for important information about properly valuing your donated items.

Clothing, Girl's

Description	High* Good Condition	Average* Fair Condition	Low* Poor Condition	Total
Pants				
Fleece	_____$6.00	_____$5.00	_____$2.00	_____
Nylon	_____$9.00	_____$5.00	_____$2.00	_____
Shirts				
Sweatshirt Long-Sleeve	_____$10.00	_____$6.00	_____$2.00	_____
Sweatshirt Short-Sleeve	_____$8.00	_____$3.00	_____$2.00	_____
Shorts				
Fleece	_____$6.00	_____$4.00	_____$1.00	_____
Nylon	_____$6.00	_____$4.00	_____$1.00	_____
Suits (Matching				
Pants and Top)				
Fleece	_____$9.00	_____$7.00	_____$2.00	_____
Nylon	_____$12.00	_____$8.00	_____$3.00	_____
Outerwear				
Casual Jackets				
Cloth	_____$9.00	_____$6.00	_____$2.00	_____
Other	_____$16.00	_____$10.00	_____$4.00	_____
Casual Winter Coats				
Ski	_____$17.00	_____$11.00	_____$4.00	_____
Other	_____$15.00	_____$12.00	_____$4.00	_____
Dress Jackets	_____$14.00	_____$9.00	_____$4.00	_____
Dress Winter Coats				
All Weather	_____$36.00	_____$22.00	_____$9.00	_____
Ear Muffs	_____$6.00	_____$3.00	_____$1.00	_____
Rainwear				
Coat	_____$11.00	_____$7.00	_____$3.00	_____
Ski Bibs	_____$9.00	_____$4.00	_____$2.00	_____
Shoes and Boots				
Boot Snow	_____$8.00	_____$6.00	_____$2.00	_____
Casual				
Shoe Leather Slip-On	_____$7.00	_____$6.00	_____$2.00	_____
Shoe Leather w/Laces	_____$10.00	_____$7.00	_____$2.00	_____

See pages 12 & 13 for important information about properly valuing your donated items.

Clothing, Girl's

Description	High* Good Condition	Average* Fair Condition	Low* Poor Condition	Total
Dress				
Shoe Leather Slip-On	_____ $10.50	_____ $7.00	_____ $3.00	_____
Shoe Leather w/Laces	_____ $12.00	_____ $7.00	_____ $3.00	_____
Sandals	_____ $8.00	_____ $5.00	_____ $2.00	_____
Slippers	_____ $5.00	_____ $3.00	_____ $1.00	_____
Sport				
Sneaker Cloth	_____ $7.00	_____ $5.00	_____ $2.00	_____
Sneaker Leather	_____ $15.00	_____ $9.00	_____ $4.00	_____
Skirts				
Jumpers				
Casual	_____ $9.00	_____ $5.00	_____ $2.00	_____
Dress	_____ $5.00	_____ $4.00	_____ $1.00	_____
Regular				
Denim	_____ $6.00	_____ $4.00	_____ $2.00	_____
Other	_____ $7.00	_____ $5.00	_____ $2.00	_____
Slacks and Pants				
Casual				
Corduroy	_____ $10.00	_____ $6.00	_____ $3.00	_____
Denim	_____ $10.00	_____ $7.00	_____ $2.00	_____
Other	_____ $8.00	_____ $5.00	_____ $2.00	_____
Dress	_____ $10.00	_____ $6.00	_____ $2.00	_____
Summerwear				
Shorts				
Denim	_____ $6.00	_____ $4.00	_____ $2.00	_____
Other	_____ $7.00	_____ $5.00	_____ $2.00	_____
Swimwear				
One-Piece	_____ $6.00	_____ $4.00	_____ $1.00	_____
Two-Piece	_____ $5.00	_____ $4.00	_____ $1.00	_____
Tops				
T-Shirt	_____ $6.00	_____ $4.00	_____ $2.00	_____
Tank	_____ $8.00	_____ $4.00	_____ $1.00	_____
Other	_____ $7.00	_____ $4.00	_____ $1.00	_____

See pages 12 & 13 for important information about properly valuing your donated items.

Clothing, Girl's

Description	High* Good Condition	Average* Fair Condition	Low* Poor Condition	Total
Sweaters				
Casual				
Cardigan	_____ $8.00	_____ $6.00	_____ $2.00	_____
Pullover Long-Sleeve	_____ $8.00	_____ $5.00	_____ $2.00	_____
V-Neck	_____ $9.00	_____ $5.00	_____ $2.00	_____
Vest	_____ $7.00	_____ $4.00	_____ $2.00	_____
Dress				
Cardigan	_____ $8.00	_____ $6.00	_____ $2.00	_____
Pullover Long-Sleeve	_____ $9.00	_____ $5.00	_____ $2.00	_____
V-Neck	_____ $9.00	_____ $4.00	_____ $1.00	_____
Vest	_____ $4.00	_____ $4.00	_____ $1.00	_____
Undergarments				
Night Shirt	_____ $4.00	_____ $3.00	_____ $1.00	_____
Nightgown	_____ $6.00	_____ $4.00	_____ $2.00	_____
Pajamas	_____ $5.00	_____ $4.00	_____ $1.00	_____
Robe	_____ $6.00	_____ $4.00	_____ $2.00	_____
Slips				
Camisole	_____ $7.00	_____ $4.00	_____ $1.00	_____
Full	_____ $3.00	_____ $2.50	_____ $1.00	_____
Half	_____ $2.00	_____ $1.50	_____ $0.50	_____
Socks (Pair)				
Dress	_____ $2.00	_____ $1.00	_____ $0.50	_____
Other	_____ $2.00	_____ $1.00	_____ $0.50	_____
TOTAL CLOTHING, GIRL'S				$

See pages 12 & 13 for important information about properly valuing your donated items.

Clothing, Infant's

Description	High* Good Condition	Average* Fair Condition	Low* Poor Condition	Total
Bedding				
Afghan	_____ $7.00	_____ $4.00	_____ $2.00	_____
Blankets	_____ $4.00	_____ $3.00	_____ $1.00	_____
Quilt	_____ $16.00	_____ $13.00	_____ $4.00	_____
Receiving Blanket	_____ $2.50	_____ $2.00	_____ $1.00	_____
Sheets Set	_____ $5.00	_____ $3.00	_____ $1.00	_____
Dresses				
Casual	_____ $9.00	_____ $6.00	_____ $2.00	_____
Dress	_____ $10.00	_____ $6.00	_____ $3.00	_____
Outerwear				
Caps	_____ $3.00	_____ $2.00	_____ $1.00	_____
Coats Winter	_____ $18.00	_____ $10.00	_____ $5.00	_____
Gloves and Mittens	_____ $2.50	_____ $1.50	_____ $1.00	_____
Jacket	_____ $8.00	_____ $6.00	_____ $2.00	_____
Snowsuits	_____ $17.00	_____ $11.00	_____ $4.00	_____
Stocking Cap	_____ $4.00	_____ $2.00	_____ $1.00	_____
Pants				
Casual	_____ $5.00	_____ $3.00	_____ $1.00	_____
Shirts				
Long-Sleeve	_____ $4.00	_____ $3.00	_____ $1.00	_____
Short-Sleeve	_____ $5.00	_____ $3.00	_____ $1.00	_____
T-Shirt	_____ $4.00	_____ $3.00	_____ $1.00	_____
Tank	_____ $5.00	_____ $3.00	_____ $1.00	_____
Shoes and Boots				
Shoes	_____ $5.00	_____ $3.00	_____ $1.00	_____

See pages 12 & 13 for important information about properly valuing your donated items.

Clothing, Infant's

Description	High* Good Condition	Average* Fair Condition	Low* Poor Condition	Total
Sleepwear				
Gowns	_____$5.00	_____$3.00	_____$1.00	_____
Sleeper w/Feet	_____$5.00	_____$4.00	_____$1.00	_____
Sleeper w/o Feet	_____$6.00	_____$4.00	_____$1.00	_____
Summerwear				
Play Suits	_____$8.00	_____$5.00	_____$2.00	_____
Shorts	_____$5.00	_____$3.00	_____$1.00	_____
Swimwear	_____$5.00	_____$4.00	_____$1.00	_____
Sweaters				
Cardigan	_____$9.00	_____$6.00	_____$2.00	_____
Pullover Long-Sleeve	_____$8.00	_____$4.00	_____$2.00	_____
Undergarments				
Booties	_____$3.00	_____$2.00	_____$0.50	_____
Socks (Pair)	_____$2.50	_____$1.00	_____$0.50	_____
Tights	_____$2.50	_____$2.00	_____$1.00	_____
TOTAL CLOTHING, INFANT'S			$	

*See pages 12 & 13 for important information about properly valuing your donated items.

Clothing, Men's

Description	High* Good Condition	Average* Fair Condition	Low* Poor Condition	Total
Accessories				
Belts				
Casual Leather	_____ $5.00	_____ $3.00	_____ $1.00	_____
Cloth	_____ $4.00	_____ $2.00	_____ $1.00	_____
Dress Leather	_____ $13.00	_____ $6.00	_____ $3.00	_____
Caps				
Stocking	_____ $9.00	_____ $6.00	_____ $1.00	_____
Summer	_____ $5.00	_____ $3.00	_____ $1.00	_____
Sun Visor	_____ $7.00	_____ $2.00	_____ $1.00	_____
Winter	_____ $16.00	_____ $9.00	_____ $2.00	_____
Handkerchiefs	_____ $3.50	_____ $2.50	_____ $1.00	_____
Hats				
Cowboy	_____ $23.00	_____ $11.00	_____ $4.00	_____
Dress	_____ $14.00	_____ $8.00	_____ $2.00	_____
Scarves				
Dress	_____ $15.00	_____ $11.00	_____ $4.00	_____
Other	_____ $6.00	_____ $3.00	_____ $1.00	_____
Suspenders				
Button-On	_____ $5.00	_____ $4.00	_____ $1.00	_____
Clip-On	_____ $5.00	_____ $3.00	_____ $1.00	_____
Ties				
Clip-On	_____ $4.00	_____ $3.00	_____ $1.00	_____
Silk	_____ $6.00	_____ $4.00	_____ $1.00	_____
Other	_____ $5.00	_____ $3.00	_____ $1.00	_____
Exercise				
Jackets				
Fleece Insulated w/Hood	_____ $19.00	_____ $6.00	_____ $3.00	_____
Fleece w/Hood	_____ $11.00	_____ $6.00	_____ $3.00	_____
Nylon	_____ $13.00	_____ $9.00	_____ $3.00	_____
Pants				
Fleece	_____ $4.00	_____ $3.00	_____ $1.00	_____
Nylon	_____ $9.00	_____ $6.00	_____ $2.00	_____

*See pages 12 & 13 for important information about properly valuing your donated items.

Clothing, Men's

Description	High* Good Condition	Average* Fair Condition	Low* Poor Condition	Total
Shirts				
Nylon Long-Sleeve	_____$13.00	_____$9.00	_____$2.00	_____
Sweatshirt Long-Sleeve	_____$10.00	_____$6.00	_____$2.00	_____
Sweatshirt Short-Sleeve	_____$11.00	_____$6.00	_____$3.00	_____
Shorts				
Fleece	_____$9.00	_____$5.00	_____$1.00	_____
Nylon	_____$4.00	_____$3.00	_____$1.00	_____
Suits (Matching Pants and Top)				
Fleece	_____$13.00	_____$8.00	_____$3.00	_____
Nylon	_____$21.00	_____$14.00	_____$5.00	_____
Outerwear				
Casual Jackets				
Cloth	_____$21.00	_____$13.00	_____$5.00	_____
Nylon	_____$12.00	_____$9.00	_____$3.00	_____
Casual Winter Coats				
Ski	_____$39.00	_____$21.00	_____$10.00	_____
Other	_____$30.00	_____$18.00	_____$8.00	_____
Coveralls	_____$30.00	_____$18.00	_____$8.00	_____
Dress Jackets				
Wool	_____$32.00	_____$17.00	_____$5.00	_____
Dress Winter Coats				
All Weather	_____$43.00	_____$28.00	_____$11.00	_____
Wool	_____$40.00	_____$20.00	_____$6.00	_____
Other	_____$33.00	_____$26.00	_____$6.00	_____
Gloves				
Dress	_____$10.00	_____$5.00	_____$2.00	_____
Leather Coats				
Casual	_____$86.00	_____$39.00	_____$19.00	_____
Dress	_____$55.00	_____$28.00	_____$8.00	_____
Rainwear				
Coat	_____$33.00	_____$28.00	_____$5.00	_____

*See pages 12 & 13 for important information about properly valuing your donated items.

Clothing, Men's

Description	High* Good Condition	Average* Fair Condition	Low* Poor Condition	Total
Ski Bibs	____$26.00	____$11.00	____$6.00	_____
Snow Mobile Outfit	____$43.00	____$13.00	____$6.00	_____
Vests				
Suede	____$6.00	____$5.00	____$1.00	_____
Winter	____$9.00	____$6.00	____$2.00	_____
## Shirts				
Casual				
Long-Sleeve	____$9.00	____$5.00	____$2.00	_____
Short-Sleeve	____$6.00	____$4.00	____$2.00	_____
Turtleneck	____$8.00	____$5.00	____$2.00	_____
Dress				
Long-Sleeve	____$9.00	____$6.00	____$2.00	_____
Short-Sleeve	____$8.00	____$5.00	____$2.00	_____
Sport				
Pullover Long-Sleeve	____$8.50	____$6.00	____$2.00	_____
Pullover Short-Sleeve	____$8.00	____$5.00	____$2.00	_____
Work				
Long-Sleeve	____$9.00	____$6.00	____$2.00	_____
Short-Sleeve	____$6.00	____$4.00	____$1.00	_____
## Shoes and Boots				
Boots Snow	____$7.00	____$6.00	____$2.00	_____
Casual				
Boot Slip-On	____$31.00	____$16.00	____$8.00	_____
Boot Western	____$21.00	____$15.00	____$5.00	_____
Shoe Slip-On	____$8.00	____$7.00	____$2.00	_____
Shoe w/Laces	____$17.00	____$12.00	____$4.00	_____
Dress				
Boot Leather Slip-On	____$21.00	____$11.00	____$4.00	_____
Shoe Leather Slip-On	____$20.00	____$12.00	____$5.00	_____
Shoe Leather w/Laces	____$20.00	____$12.00	____$5.00	_____
Slippers	____$8.00	____$5.00	____$2.00	_____

*See pages 12 & 13 for important information about properly valuing your donated items.

Clothing, Men's

Description	High* Good Condition	Average* Fair Condition	Low* Poor Condition	Total
Sport				
Boot Hiking w/Laces	____$20.00	____$10.00	____$5.00	_____
Boot Hunting w/Laces	____$12.00	____$10.00	____$3.00	_____
Sneaker Leather	____$17.00	____$10.00	____$4.00	_____
Slacks and Pants				
Casual				
Corduroy	____$10.00	____$7.00	____$3.00	_____
Denim	____$9.00	____$6.00	____$2.00	_____
Other	____$12.00	____$8.00	____$3.00	_____
Dress	____$15.00	____$8.00	____$4.00	_____
Sleepwear				
Pajamas				
Matching Set	____$9.00	____$6.00	____$2.00	_____
Robe	____$14.00	____$9.00	____$4.00	_____
Suits				
Casual				
Sports Coat	____$25.00	____$14.00	____$6.00	_____
Custom Tailored				
Two-Piece	____$65.00	____$38.00	____$16.00	_____
Dress				
Coat	____$27.00	____$14.00	____$7.00	_____
Slacks	____$14.00	____$8.00	____$3.00	_____
Two-Piece	____$55.00	____$31.00	____$14.00	_____
Vest	____$20.00	____$8.00	____$4.00	_____
Summerwear				
Shirts				
T-Shirt	____$5.00	____$4.00	____$1.00	_____
Tank	____$8.00	____$5.00	____$2.00	_____
Shorts				
Denim	____$7.00	____$5.00	____$2.00	_____
Other	____$7.00	____$4.00	____$2.00	_____

*See pages 12 & 13 for important information about properly valuing your donated items.

Clothing, Men's

Description	High* Good Condition	Average* Fair Condition	Low* Poor Condition	Total
Swimwear	_____$5.00	_____$3.00	_____$1.00	_____
Sweaters				
Casual				
Cardigan	_____$9.00	_____$6.00	_____2.00	_____
Pullover Long-Sleeve	_____$9.00	_____$6.00	_____$2.00	_____
Turtleneck	_____$9.00	_____$6.00	_____$2.00	_____
V-Neck	_____$13.00	_____$8.00	_____$3.00	_____
Vest	_____$7.00	_____$6.00	_____$2.00	_____
Dress				
Cardigan	_____$13.00	_____$8.00	_____$3.00	_____
Pullover Long-Sleeve	_____$21.00	_____$10.00	_____$5.00	_____
Turtleneck	_____$7.00	_____$5.00	_____$2.00	_____
V-Neck	_____$8.00	_____$6.00	_____$2.00	_____
Vest	_____$7.00	_____$6.00	_____$2.00	_____
Undergarments				
Pants				
Insulated	_____$5.00	_____$4.00	_____$1.00	_____
Shirts				
Insulated Long-Sleeve	_____$6.00	_____$4.00	_____$1.00	_____
T-Shirt	_____$6.00	_____$5.00	_____$1.00	_____
Socks (Pair)				
Dress	_____$1.50	_____$1.00	_____$0.50	_____
Other	_____$1.00	_____$0.50	_____$0.25	_____
TOTAL CLOTHING, MEN'S			$	

Try ItsDeductible Software!

• Direct import into TurboTax® Software
• Quick Search for items
• Receipt and report printing
• Tips and Internet links

It even completes IRS Form 8283, automatically!

www.ItsDeductible.com $19.95

See pages 12 & 13 for important information about properly valuing your donated items.

Clothing, Toddler's

Description	High* Good Condition	Average* Fair Condition	Low* Poor Condition	Total
Dresses				
Casual	_____ $10.00	_____ $7.00	_____ $2.00	_____
Dress	_____ $15.00	_____ $10.00	_____ $4.00	_____
Exercise				
Jackets				
Fleece w/Hood	_____ $7.00	_____ $5.00	_____ $2.00	_____
Pants				
Fleece	_____ $6.00	_____ $4.00	_____ $1.00	_____
Nylon	_____ $7.00	_____ $5.00	_____ $2.00	_____
Shirts				
Nylon	_____ $7.00	_____ $3.00	_____ $1.00	_____
Sweatshirt	_____ $5.00	_____ $3.00	_____ $1.00	_____
Suits (Matching Pants and Top)				
Fleece	_____ $9.00	_____ $5.00	_____ $2.00	_____
Nylon	_____ $11.00	_____ $7.00	_____ $3.00	_____
Outerwear				
Bib Overalls				
Corduroy	_____ $6.00	_____ $4.00	_____ $1.00	_____
Denim	_____ $8.00	_____ $5.00	_____ $2.00	_____
Other	_____ $11.00	_____ $7.00	_____ $3.00	_____
Cap	_____ $5.00	_____ $3.00	_____ $1.00	_____
Gloves	_____ $2.00	_____ $2.00	_____ $1.00	_____
Jackets				
Casual	_____ $8.00	_____ $5.00	_____ $2.00	_____
Dress	_____ $17.00	_____ $8.00	_____ $4.00	_____
Raincoat	_____ $12.00	_____ $7.00	_____ $3.00	_____
Snowsuit	_____ $15.00	_____ $10.00	_____ $4.00	_____
Sweaters	_____ $9.00	_____ $5.00	_____ $2.00	_____
Winter Coats				
Casual	_____ $19.00	_____ $13.00	_____ $5.00	_____
Dress	_____ $14.00	_____ $10.00	_____ $4.00	_____

See pages 12 & 13 for important information about properly valuing your donated items.

Clothing, Toddler's

Description	High* Good Condition	Average* Fair Condition	Low* Poor Condition	Total
Pants				
Denim	_____ $8.00	_____ $6.00	_____ $2.00	_____
Other	_____ $8.00	_____ $4.00	_____ $2.00	_____
Shirts and Blouses				
Long-Sleeve	_____ $5.00	_____ $3.00	_____ $1.00	_____
Short-Sleeve	_____ $7.00	_____ $4.00	_____ $1.00	_____
Turtleneck	_____ $5.00	_____ $4.00	_____ $1.00	_____
Shoes and Boots				
Boots Leather	_____ $10.00	_____ $6.00	_____ $2.00	_____
Boots Snow	_____ $8.00	_____ $7.00	_____ $2.00	_____
Shoe Leather	_____ $9.00	_____ $6.00	_____ $2.00	_____
Shoe Other	_____ $6.00	_____ $4.00	_____ $1.00	_____
Slippers	_____ $8.00	_____ $4.00	_____ $2.00	_____
Sneaker Leather	_____ $8.00	_____ $4.00	_____ $2.00	_____
Skirts				
Casual	_____ $5.00	_____ $4.00	_____ $1.00	_____
Sleepwear				
Pajamas				
Gown	_____ $4.00	_____ $3.00	_____ $1.00	_____
Matching Set	_____ $4.00	_____ $3.00	_____ $1.00	_____
Sleepers w/Feet	_____ $5.00	_____ $4.00	_____ $1.00	_____
Sleepers w/o Feet	_____ $5.00	_____ $4.00	_____ $1.00	_____
Suits				
Dress	_____ $11.00	_____ $7.00	_____ $3.00	_____
Summerwear				
Shirts				
T-Shirt	_____ $4.00	_____ $3.00	_____ $1.00	_____
Tank	_____ $5.00	_____ $3.00	_____ $1.00	_____

*See pages 12 & 13 for important information about properly valuing your donated items.

Clothing, Toddler's

Description	High* Good Condition	Average* Fair Condition	Low* Poor Condition	Total
Shorts				
Denim	_____ $6.00	_____ $4.00	_____ $1.00	_____
Other	_____ $8.00	_____ $4.00	_____ $2.00	_____
Swimsuits	_____ $6.00	_____ $4.00	_____ $1.00	_____
Sweaters				
Cardigan	_____ $10.00	_____ $6.00	_____ $2.00	_____
Pullover Long-Sleeve	_____ $8.00	_____ $5.00	_____ $2.00	_____
Vest	_____ $5.00	_____ $4.00	_____ $1.00	_____
Undergarments				
Plastic Pants	_____ $2.00	_____ $1.00	_____ $0.50	_____
Socks (Pair)				
Dress	_____ $2.00	_____ $1.00	_____ $0.50	_____
Other	_____ $1.00	_____ $1.00	_____ $0.50	_____
Tights	_____ $3.00	_____ $1.00	_____ $0.50	_____
TOTAL CLOTHING, TODDLER'S			$	

See pages 12 & 13 for important information about properly valuing your donated items.

Clothing, Women's

Description	High* Good Condition	Average* Fair Condition	Low* Poor Condition	Total
Accessories				
Belts				
Leather	_____ $12.00	_____ $6.00	_____ $3.00	_____
Other	_____ $6.00	_____ $4.00	_____ $1.00	_____
Gloves				
Casual	_____ $9.00	_____ $5.00	_____ $2.00	_____
Dress	_____ $13.00	_____ $7.00	_____ $3.00	_____
Mittens	_____ $9.00	_____ $3.00	_____ $1.00	_____
Purses				
Dress	_____ $39.00	_____ $18.00	_____ $9.00	_____
Leather	_____ $28.00	_____ $13.00	_____ $6.00	_____
Other	_____ $21.00	_____ $10.00	_____ $5.00	_____
Scarves				
Dress	_____ $17.00	_____ $9.00	_____ $4.00	_____
Other	_____ $14.00	_____ $5.00	_____ $2.00	_____
Blouses and Shirts				
Casual				
Long-Sleeve	_____ $15.00	_____ $8.00	_____ $4.00	_____
Short-Sleeve	_____ $12.00	_____ $7.00	_____ $3.00	_____
Turtleneck	_____ $15.00	_____ $7.00	_____ $4.00	_____
Dress				
Long-Sleeve	_____ $18.00	_____ $10.00	_____ $5.00	_____
Short-Sleeve	_____ $16.00	_____ $8.00	_____ $4.00	_____
Dresses				
Casual	_____ $28.00	_____ $16.00	_____ $7.00	_____
Dress	_____ $30.00	_____ $18.00	_____ $7.00	_____
Summer	_____ $20.00	_____ $13.00	_____ $5.00	_____
Wool	_____ $38.00	_____ $22.00	_____ $9.00	_____

*See pages 12 & 13 for important information about properly valuing your donated items.

Clothing, Women's

Description	High* Good Condition	Average* Fair Condition	Low* Poor Condition	Total
Exercise				
Jackets				
Fleece w/Hood	_____ $15.00	_____ $9.00	_____ $4.00	_____
Nylon w/Hood	_____ $20.00	_____ $12.00	_____ $5.00	_____
Nylon Insulated w/Hood	_____ $29.00	_____ $22.00	_____ $7.00	_____
Leotards	_____ $4.00	_____ $3.50	_____ $1.00	
Pants				
Fleece	_____ $18.00	_____ $7.00	_____ $4.00	_____
Nylon	_____ $15.00	_____ $7.00	_____ $4.00	_____
Shirts				
Fleece Long-Sleeve	_____ $11.00	_____ $5.00	_____ $3.00	_____
Fleece Short-Sleeve	_____ $9.00	_____ $5.00	_____ $2.00	_____
Nylon Long-Sleeve w/Zipper	_____ $10.00	_____ $5.00	_____ $3.00	_____
Shorts				
Fleece	_____ $6.00	_____ $4.00	_____ $2.00	_____
Nylon	_____ $4.00	_____ $3.00	_____ $1.00	_____
Formals				
Long	_____ $112.00	_____ $62.00	_____ $28.00	_____
Short	_____ $46.00	_____ $34.00	_____ $11.00	_____
Wedding Gown	_____ $180.00	_____ $124.00	_____ $45.00	_____
Maternity				
Casual Tops				
Long-Sleeve	_____ $13.00	_____ $9.00	_____ $3.00	_____
Short-Sleeve	_____ $9.00	_____ $6.00	_____ $2.00	_____
Dress Tops				
Long-Sleeve	_____ $15.00	_____ $11.00	_____ $4.00	_____
Short-Sleeve	_____ $17.00	_____ $9.00	_____ $4.00	_____
Dresses				
Casual	_____ $16.00	_____ $10.00	_____ $4.00	_____
Dress	_____ $37.00	_____ $19.00	_____ $9.00	_____

See pages 12 & 13 for important information about properly valuing your donated items.

Clothing, Women's

Description	High* Good Condition	Average* Fair Condition	Low* Poor Condition	Total
Skirts	____$9.00	____$8.00	____$2.00	_____
Slacks				
Casual	____$11.00	____$8.00	____$3.00	_____
Dress	____$14.00	____$8.00	____$3.00	_____
Jumpers	____$25.00	____$18.00	____$6.00	_____
Suits				
Skirt and Jacket	____$41.00	____$29.00	____$10.00	_____
Slacks and Jacket	____$38.00	____$31.00	____$10.00	_____
Outerwear				
Casual Jackets				
Cloth	____$29.00	____$18.00	____$7.00	_____
Nylon	____$24.00	____$16.00	____$6.00	_____
Casual Winter Coats				
Ski	____$29.00	____$16.00	____$7.00	_____
Other	____$32.00	____$16.00	____$8.00	_____
Dress Jackets				
Cloth	____$30.00	____$17.00	____$7.00	_____
Wool	____$25.00	____$18.00	____$6.00	_____
Dress Winter Coats				
All Weather	____$47.00	____$31.00	____$12.00	_____
Wool Cape	____$57.00	____$35.00	____$14.00	_____
Wool Coat	____$46.00	____$29.00	____$12.00	_____
Other	____$75.00	____$41.00	____$19.00	_____
Leather Coats				
Casual	____$58.00	____$35.00	____$14.00	_____
Dress	____$73.00	____$40.00	____$17.00	_____
Rainwear				
Coat	____$35.00	____$20.00	____$9.00	_____
Shoes and Boots				
Boot Snow	____$11.00	____$6.00	____$3.00	_____

*See pages 12 & 13 for important information about properly valuing your donated items.

Clothing, Women's

Description	High* Good Condition	Average* Fair Condition	Low* Poor Condition	Total
Casual				
Boot Leather	$23.00	$13.00	$6.00	
Boot Other	$39.00	$25.00	$10.00	
Shoe Slip-On	$18.00	$10.00	$4.00	
Shoe w/Laces	$14.00	$8.00	$3.00	
Dress				
Boot Leather	$22.00	$12.00	$5.00	
Boot Other	$17.00	$10.00	$4.00	
Pumps Leather	$23.00	$12.00	$6.00	
Shoe Leather	$18.00	$10.00	$4.00	
Shoe Other	$21.00	$13.00	$5.00	
Sandals				
Leather	$14.00	$10.00	$4.00	
Moccasins	$16.00	$9.00	$2.00	
Slippers	$10.00	$5.00	$2.00	
Sport				
Sneaker Cloth	$11.00	$7.00	$3.00	
Sneaker Leather	$16.00	$8.00	$4.00	
Tap	$8.00	$7.00	$2.00	
Water Socks	$17.00	$7.00	$4.00	
Skirts				
Jumpers				
Casual	$26.00	$16.00	$6.00	
Dress	$16.00	$10.00	$4.00	
Mini				
Denim	$12.00	$8.00	$3.00	
Leather	$39.00	$24.00	$10.00	
Other	$15.00	$9.00	$4.00	
Regular				
Corduroy	$16.00	$10.00	$4.00	
Denim	$17.00	$11.00	$4.00	
Other	$18.00	$10.00	$4.00	

See pages 12 & 13 for important information about properly valuing your donated items.

Clothing, Women's

Description	High* Good Condition	Average* Fair Condition	Low* Poor Condition	Total
Slacks and Pants				
Casual				
Corduroy	_____$17.00	_____$11.00	_____$4.00	_____
Denim	_____$12.00	_____$9.00	_____$3.00	_____
Other	_____$15.00	_____$9.00	_____$4.00	_____
Dress	_____$19.00	_____$12.00	_____$5.00	_____
Sleepwear				
Night Shirt	_____$15.00	_____$7.00	_____$4.00	_____
Nightgown	_____$16.00	_____$9.00	_____$4.00	_____
Pajamas				
Matching Set	_____$18.00	_____$10.00	_____$4.00	_____
Robe	_____$22.00	_____$11.00	_____$5.00	_____
Teddies	_____$11.00	_____$7.00	_____$3.00	_____
Suits				
Custom Tailored				
Skirt and Jacket	_____$44.00	_____$22.00	_____$9.00	_____
Slacks and Jacket	_____$49.00	_____$31.00	_____$12.00	_____
Jacket	_____$33.00	_____$19.00	_____$8.00	_____
Skirt	_____$21.00	_____$15.00	_____$5.00	_____
Skirt and Jacket	_____$52.00	_____$32.00	_____$13.00	_____
Slacks	_____$19.00	_____$14.00	_____$5.00	_____
Slacks and Jacket	_____$70.00	_____$40.00	_____$17.00	_____
Summerwear				
Shorts				
Denim	_____$12.00	_____$6.00	_____$3.00	_____
Other	_____$13.00	_____$6.00	_____$3.00	_____
Swimsuits				
Maternity	_____$18.00	_____$11.00	_____$5.00	_____
One-Piece	_____$22.00	_____$9.00	_____$4.00	_____
Two-Piece	_____$8.00	_____$5.00	_____$2.00	_____

*See pages 12 & 13 for important information about properly valuing your donated items.

Clothing, Women's

Description	High* Good Condition	Average* Fair Condition	Low* Poor Condition	Total
Tops				
T-Shirt	_____$9.00	_____$6.00	_____$2.00	_____
Tank	_____$11.00	_____$8.00	_____$3.00	_____
Other	_____$17.00	_____$8.00	_____$4.00	_____
Sweaters				
Casual				
Cardigan	_____$18.00	_____$10.00	_____$4.00	_____
Pullover Long-Sleeve	_____$20.00	_____$11.00	_____$5.00	_____
Turtleneck	_____$19.00	_____$11.00	_____$5.00	_____
Vest	_____$16.00	_____$9.00	_____$4.00	_____
Dress				
Cardigan	_____$27.00	_____$15.00	_____$7.00	_____
Pullover Long-Sleeve	_____$30.00	_____$17.00	_____$8.00	_____
Turtleneck	_____$19.00	_____$10.00	_____$5.00	_____
Vest	_____$15.00	_____$10.00	_____$4.00	_____
V-Neck	_____$24.00	_____$14.00	_____$6.00	_____
Undergarments				
Bras				
Regular	_____$7.00	_____$4.00	_____$2.00	_____
Sport	_____$4.00	_____$3.00	_____$1.00	_____
Girdle	_____$15.00	_____$9.00	_____$4.00	_____
Slips				
Camisole	_____$8.00	_____$5.00	_____$2.00	_____
Full	_____$8.00	_____$4.00	_____$2.00	_____
Half	_____$5.00	_____$3.00	_____$1.00	_____
Socks (Pair)				
Dress	_____$1.00	_____$0.50	_____$0.25	_____
Other	_____$2.00	_____$1.00	_____$0.50	_____
Tights	_____$2.00	_____$1.50	_____$0.50	_____
TOTAL CLOTHING, WOMEN'S			$	

See pages 12 & 13 for important information about properly valuing your donated items.

Designer Clothing, Men's

Description	High* Good Condition	Average* Fair Condition	Low* Poor Condition	Total
Accessories				
Belts				
Casual	___$31.00	___$24.00	___$3.00	_____
Leather	___$29.00	___$10.00	___$4.00	_____
Hats				
Cowboy	___$89.00	___$66.00	___$22.00	_____
Dress	___$23.00	___$14.00	___$6.00	_____
Ties				
Clip-on	___$5.00	___$3.00	___$1.00	_____
Silk	___$26.00	___$20.00	___$7.00	_____
Other	___$13.00	___$7.00	___$1.00	_____
Exercise				
Jackets				
Fleece	___$19.00	___$13.00	___$5.00	_____
Nylon	___$14.00	___$10.00	___$4.00	_____
Pants				
Fleece	___$19.00	___$12.00	___$5.00	_____
Nylon	___$14.00	___$10.00	___$3.00	_____
Shirts				
Nylon Long-Sleeve	___$17.00	___$13.00	___$4.00	_____
Sweatshirt Long-Sleeve	___$29.00	___$12.00	___$4.00	_____
Shorts				
Fleece	___$12.00	___$9.00	___$3.00	_____
Nylon	___$12.00	___$8.00	___$3.00	_____
Suits (Matching Pants and Top)				
Fleece	___$71.00	___$45.00	___$11.00	_____
Nylon	___$23.00	___$17.00	___$6.00	_____
Outerwear				
Casual Jackets				
Cloth	___$33.00	___$21.00	___$8.00	_____
Nylon	___$28.00	___$19.00	___$7.00	_____

See pages 12 & 13 for important information about properly valuing your donated items.

Designer Clothing, Men's

Description	High* Good Condition	Average* Fair Condition	Low* Poor Condition	Total
Casual Winter Coats				
Ski	$76.00	$46.00	$19.00	
Other	$58.00	$39.00	$14.00	
Dress Jackets	$149.00	$113.00	$37.00	
Dress Winter Coats				
All Weather	$99.00	$62.00	$25.00	
Wool	$64.00	$40.00	$16.00	
Other	$80.00	$42.00	$20.00	
Leather Coats				
Casual	$103.00	$55.00	$26.00	
Dress	$224.00	$144.00	$56.00	
Rainwear	$35.00	$28.00	$5.00	
Vests				
Down	$22.00	$15.00	$6.00	
Suede	$24.00	$16.00	$6.00	
Shirts				
Casual				
Long-Sleeve	$19.00	$10.00	$5.00	
Short-Sleeve	$12.00	$7.00	$3.00	
Turtleneck	$16.00	$13.00	$4.00	
Dress				
Long-Sleeve	$24.00	$14.00	$6.00	
Short-Sleeve	$19.00	$16.00	$5.00	
Sport				
Pullover Long-Sleeve	$17.00	$7.00	$4.00	
Pullover Short-Sleeve	$19.00	$7.00	$5.00	
Shoes and Boots				
Casual				
Shoes Slip-On	$44.00	$29.00	$11.00	
Shoes w/Laces	$42.00	$36.00	$11.00	
Dress				
Boots Leather	$59.00	$40.00	$15.00	
Shoes Slip-On	$38.00	$35.00	$10.00	
Shoes w/Laces	$41.00	$37.00	$10.00	

See pages 12 & 13 for important information about properly valuing your donated items.

Designer Clothing, Men's

Description	High* Good Condition	Average* Fair Condition	Low* Poor Condition	Total
Sport				
Boots Hiking	____$49.00	____$33.00	____$12.00	_____
Boots Hunting	____$48.00	____$10.00	____$4.00	_____
Boots Snow	____$30.00	____$6.00	____$3.00	_____
Sneakers Leather	____$31.00	____$25.00	____$8.00	_____
Sneakers Other	____$22.00	____$17.00	____$5.00	_____
Slacks and Pants				
Casual				
Corduroy	____$22.00	____$11.00	____$5.00	_____
Denim	____$27.00	____$13.00	____$7.00	_____
Other	____$21.00	____$11.00	____$5.00	_____
Dress	____$39.00	____$28.00	____$10.00	_____
Sleepwear				
Pajamas				
Matching Set	____$23.00	____$9.00	____$4.00	_____
Robe	____$11.00	____$8.00	____$3.00	_____
Suits				
Casual				
Sport Coat	____$124.00	____$83.00	____$31.00	_____
Custom Tailored				
Two-Piece	____$296.00	____$179.00	____$74.00	_____
Dress				
Coat	____$169.00	____$115.00	____$42.00	_____
Slacks	____$47.00	____$35.00	____$12.00	_____
Two-Piece	____$280.00	____$140.00	____$50.00	_____
Vest	____$39.00	____$25.00	____$10.00	_____
Summerwear				
Shirts				
T-Shirt	____$13.00	____$7.00	____$3.00	_____
Shorts				
Denim	____$22.00	____$12.00	____$5.00	_____
Other	____$10.00	____$5.00	____$2.00	_____

See pages 12 & 13 for important information about properly valuing your donated items.

ItsDeductible™
Turning Donations Into Dollars

Designer Clothing, Men's

Description	High* Good Condition	Average* Fair Condition	Low* Poor Condition	Total
Sweaters				
Casual				
Cardigan	_____$13.00	_____$8.00	_____$3.00	_____
Pullover Long-Sleeve	_____$14.00	_____$9.00	_____$4.00	_____
Turtleneck	_____$16.00	_____$11.00	_____$4.00	_____
V-Neck	_____$11.00	_____$8.00	_____$3.00	_____
Vest	_____$20.00	_____$7.00	_____$5.00	_____
Dress				
Cardigan	_____$44.00	_____$27.00	_____$11.00	_____
Pullover Long-Sleeve	_____$38.00	_____$24.00	_____$9.00	_____
Turtleneck	_____$39.00	_____$31.00	_____$10.00	_____
V-Neck	_____$38.00	_____$25.00	_____$9.00	_____
Vest	_____$20.00	_____$13.00	_____$5.00	_____

TOTAL DESIGNER CLOTHING, MEN'S	**$**

See pages 12 & 13 for important information about properly valuing your donated items.

Designer Clothing, Women's

Description	High* Good Condition	Average* Fair Condition	Low* Poor Condition	Total
Accessories				
Belts				
Leather	____$33.00	____$21.00	____$8.00	_____
Other	____$27.00	____$14.00	____$7.00	_____
Gloves				
Dress	____$12.00	____$9.00	____$3.00	_____
Leather	____$18.00	____$9.00	____$3.00	_____
Purses				
Dress	____$103.00	____$48.00	____$20.00	_____
Leather	____$72.00	____$38.00	____$18.00	_____
Other	____$38.00	____$24.00	____$9.00	_____
Scarves				
Dress	____$12.00	____$10.00	____$3.00	_____
Other	____$18.00	____$13.00	____$5.00	_____
Blouses and Shirts				
Casual				
Long-Sleeve	____$33.00	____$16.00	____$8.00	_____
Short-Sleeve	____$24.00	____$12.00	____$6.00	_____
Turtleneck	____$20.00	____$16.00	____$5.00	_____
Dress				
Long-Sleeve	____$39.00	____$21.00	____$10.00	_____
Short-Sleeve	____$31.00	____$21.00	____$8.00	_____
Dresses				
Casual	____$47.00	____$31.00	____$12.00	_____
Dress	____$70.00	____$40.00	____$18.00	_____
Summer	____$42.00	____$23.00	____$10.00	_____
Wool	____$30.00	____$24.00	____$8.00	_____
Exercise				
Jackets				
Fleece	____$15.00	____$13.00	____$4.00	_____
Nylon	____$14.00	____$10.00	____$4.00	_____

*See pages 12 & 13 for important information about properly valuing your donated items.

Designer Clothing, Women's

Description	High* Good Condition	Average* Fair Condition	Low* Poor Condition	Total
Pants				
Fleece	$15.00	$12.00	$4.00	
Nylon	$13.00	$10.00	$3.00	
Shirts				
Sweatshirt Long-Sleeve	$13.00	$9.00	$3.00	
Sweatshirt Short-Sleeve	$10.00	$9.00	$3.00	
Shorts				
Fleece	$8.00	$6.00	$2.00	
Nylon	$9.00	$6.00	$2.00	
Formals				
Long	$218.00	$106.00	$54.00	
Short	$115.00	$64.00	$29.00	
Wedding Gown	$300.00	$110.00	$75.00	
Jumpers				
Casual	$39.00	$34.00	$10.00	
Dress	$40.00	$35.00	$10.00	
Outerwear				
Casual Jackets				
Cloth	$37.00	$24.00	$9.00	
Nylon	$18.00	$10.00	$5.00	
Casual Winter Coats				
Ski	$40.00	$22.00	$10.00	
Other	$36.00	$29.00	$9.00	
Dress Jackets				
Cloth	$68.00	$25.00	$10.00	
Wool	$74.00	$64.00	$19.00	
Dress Winter Coats				
All Weather	$67.00	$56.00	$17.00	
Wool	$137.00	$76.00	$34.00	
Other	$79.00	$25.00	$15.00	

See pages 12 & 13 for important information about properly valuing your donated items.

Designer Clothing, Women's

Description	High* Good Condition	Average* Fair Condition	Low* Poor Condition	Total
Leather Coats				
Casual	___$153.00	___$95.00	___$38.00	_____
Dress	___$166.00	___$130.00	___$42.00	_____
Shoes and Boots				
Casual				
Boots Leather	___$51.00	___$45.00	___$13.00	_____
Shoes Slip-On	___$37.00	___$21.00	___$9.00	_____
Shoes w/Laces	___$37.00	___$23.00	___$8.00	_____
Dress				
Boots Leather	___$84.00	___$55.00	___$21.00	_____
Boots Other	___$40.00	___$26.00	___$10.00	_____
Pumps Leather	___$37.00	___$21.00	___$9.00	_____
Shoes Leather	___$30.00	___$24.00	___$7.00	_____
Shoes Other	___$20.00	___$10.00	___$5.00	_____
Miscellaneous				
Boots Snow	___$30.00	___$26.00	___$8.00	_____
Sandals	___$32.00	___$20.00	___$8.00	_____
Sport				
Sneakers Cloth	___$24.00	___$16.00	___$6.00	_____
Sneakers Other	___$10.00	___$9.00	___$3.00	_____
Skirts				
Casual				
Corduroy	___$24.00	___$21.00	___$6.00	_____
Denim	___$19.00	___$15.00	___$5.00	_____
Other	___$29.00	___$21.00	___$7.00	_____
Mini				
Denim	___$21.00	___$15.00	___$5.00	_____
Leather	___$44.00	___$32.00	___$11.00	_____
Other	___$23.00	___$16.00	___$6.00	_____
Slacks and Pants				
Casual				
Corduroy	___$16.00	___$14.00	___$4.00	_____
Denim	___$28.00	___$19.00	___$7.00	_____

See pages 12 & 13 for important information about properly valuing your donated items.

Designer Clothing, Women's

Description	High* Good Condition	Average* Fair Condition	Low* Poor Condition	Total
Other	____$30.00	____$19.00	____$8.00	_____
Dress	____$37.00	____$24.00	____$9.00	_____
Sleepwear				
Nightgown	____$15.00	____$10.00	____$4.00	_____
Pajamas				
Matching Set	____$19.00	____$13.00	____$5.00	_____
Robe	____$22.00	____$14.00	____$5.00	_____
Teddies	____$21.00	____$18.00	____$5.00	_____
Suits				
Custom Tailored				
Skirt and Jacket	____$134.00	____$49.00	____$26.00	_____
Slacks and Jacket	____$127.00	____$84.00	____$32.00	_____
Jacket	____$69.00	____$35.00	____$17.00	_____
Skirt	____$51.00	____$37.00	____$13.00	_____
Skirt and Jacket	____$141.00	____$71.00	____$35.00	_____
Slacks	____$67.00	____$40.00	____$17.00	_____
Slacks and Jacket	____$135.00	____$74.00	____$34.00	_____
Summerwear				
Shorts				
Denim	____$15.00	____$10.00	____$4.00	_____
Other	____$12.00	____$8.00	____$3.00	_____
Swimsuits				
One-Piece	____$21.00	____$13.00	____$5.00	_____
Two-Piece	____$29.00	____$16.00	____$7.00	_____
Tops				
T-Shirt	____$10.00	____$7.00	____$2.00	_____
Tank	____$15.00	____$9.00	____$4.00	_____
Other	____$19.00	____$11.00	____$5.00	_____

See pages 12 & 13 for important information about properly valuing your donated items.

Designer Clothing, Women's

Description	High* Good Condition	Average* Fair Condition	Low* Poor Condition	Total
Sweaters				
Casual				
Cardigan	____$37.00	____$21.00	____$9.00	____
Pullover	____$20.00	____$13.00	____$5.00	____
Turtleneck	____$26.00	____$17.00	____$7.00	____
V-Neck	____$25.00	____$19.00	____$6.00	____
Vest	____$23.00	____$16.00	____$6.00	____
Dress				
Cardigan	____$28.00	____$21.00	____$7.00	____
Pullover	____$20.00	____$16.00	____$5.00	____
Turtleneck	____$32.00	____$27.00	____$8.00	____
V-Neck	____$31.00	____$26.00	____$8.00	____
Vest	____$13.00	____$10.00	____$3.00	____
Undergarments				
Slips				
Camisole	____$11.00	____$7.00	____$3.00	____
Full	____$14.00	____$9.00	____$3.00	____
Half	____$10.00	____$7.00	____$3.00	____
TOTAL DESIGNER CLOTHING, WOMEN'S			$	

See pages 12 & 13 for important information about properly valuing your donated items.

Electric Appliances, Large

Description	High* Good Condition	Average* Fair Condition	Low* Poor Condition	Total
Dishwasher	___$142.00	___$78.00	___$21.00	_____
Dryer	___$157.00	___$113.00	___$91.00	_____
Freezer				
Chest	___$91.00	___$60.00	___$14.00	_____
Upright	___$95.00	___$52.00	___$14.00	_____
Microwave Oven	___$52.00	___$32.00	___$8.00	_____
Oven				
Wall	___$104.00	___$43.00	___$16.00	_____
Double Oven	___$190.00	___$100.00	___$49.00	_____
Oven/Microwave	___$225.00	___$125.00	___$20.00	_____
Refrigerator	___$189.00	___$81.00	___$28.00	_____
Stove				
Electric	___$161.00	___$136.00	___$60.00	_____
Gas	___$172.00	___$72.00	___$35.00	_____
Washer/Dryer Set	___$214.00	___$120.00	___$32.00	_____
Washing Machine	___$173.00	___$139.00	___$83.00	_____
TOTAL ELECTRIC APPLIANCES, LARGE				$

See pages 12 & 13 for important information about properly valuing your donated items.

Electric Appliances, Small

Description	High* Good Condition	Average* Fair Condition	Low* Poor Condition	Total
Air Purifier				
Name Brand	____$43.00	____$30.00	____$7.00	_____
Other	____$26.00	____$18.00	____$4.00	_____
Blender				
Name Brand	____$24.00	____$17.00	____$4.00	_____
Other	____$6.00	____$4.00	____$1.00	_____
Bread Machine				
Name Brand	____$35.00	____$24.00	____$5.00	_____
Other	____$16.00	____$11.00	____$2.00	_____
Burger Maker	____$7.00	____$5.00	____$1.00	_____
Can Opener - Electric				
Name Brand	____$14.00	____$10.00	____$2.00	_____
Other	____$5.00	____$3.00	____$1.00	_____
Cappuccino/Espresso Maker				
Name Brand	____$47.00	____$24.00	____$7.00	_____
Other	____$13.00	____$9.00	____$2.00	_____
Coffee Bean Grinder				
Name Brand	____$24.00	____$17.00	____$4.00	_____
Other	____$11.00	____$8.00	____$2.00	_____
Coffee Maker - Electric				
Name Brand	____$30.00	____$21.00	____$5.00	_____
Other	____$11.00	____$8.00	____$2.00	_____
Crock Pot	____$8.00	____$5.00	____$3.00	_____
Curling Iron	____$3.00	____$2.00	____$1.00	_____
Deep Fryer	____$42.00	____$29.00	____$6.00	_____

*See pages 12 & 13 for important information about properly valuing your donated items.

Electric Appliances, Small

Description	High* Good Condition	Average* Fair Condition	Low* Poor Condition	Total
Dehumidifier				
Name Brand	___$63.00	___$44.00	___$10.00	_____
Other	___$43.00	___$30.00	___$6.00	_____
Electric Shaver				
Name Brand	___$37.00	___$26.00	___$6.00	_____
Other	___$10.00	___$7.00	___$1.00	_____
Food Dehydrator				
Name Brand	___$31.00	___$22.00	___$5.00	_____
Other	___$15.00	___$10.00	___$2.00	_____
Food Processor				
Name Brand	___$25.00	___$15.00	___$4.00	_____
Other	___$7.00	___$4.00	___$1.00	_____
Food Steamer				
Name Brand	___$33.00	___$23.00	___$5.00	_____
Other	___$10.00	___$7.00	___$2.00	_____
George Foreman Grill				
Deluxe	___$22.00	___$15.00	___$3.00	_____
Double Champion	___$85.00	___$59.00	___$13.00	_____
Family	___$46.00	___$32.00	___$7.00	_____
Fusion	___$25.00	___$17.00	___$4.00	_____
Jumbo	___$74.00	___$52.00	___$11.00	_____
Rotisserie	___$58.00	___$41.00	___$9.00	_____
The Champ	___$16.00	___$11.00	___$2.00	_____
X-Large	___$41.00	___$28.00	___$6.00	_____
XX-Large	___$65.00	___$46.00	___$10.00	_____
Hair Blow Dryer	___$5.00	___$4.00	___$3.00	_____

*See pages 12 & 13 for important information about properly valuing your donated items.

Electric Appliances, Small

Description	High* Good Condition	Average* Fair Condition	Low* Poor Condition	Total
Ice Cream Maker				
Name Brand	$31.00	$22.00	$5.00	
Other	$8.00	$6.00	$1.00	
Iron				
Name Brand	$24.00	$17.00	$4.00	
Other	$6.00	$4.00	$1.00	
Juicer				
Name Brand	$30.00	$20.00	$5.00	
Other	$16.00	$11.00	$2.00	
Knife - Electric				
Name Brand	$24.00	$12.00	$4.00	
Other	$5.00	$3.00	$1.00	
Mixer				
Name Brand	$24.00	$12.00	$4.00	
Other	$5.00	$3.00	$1.00	
Pasta Maker				
Name Brand	$28.00	$19.00	$4.00	
Other	$16.00	$11.00	$2.00	
Popcorn Popper - Hot Air	$10.00	$7.00	$2.00	
Skillet - Electric				
Name Brand	$27.00	$19.00	$4.00	
Other	$12.00	$8.00	$2.00	
Toaster				
Name Brand	$20.00	$11.00	$3.00	
Other	$6.00	$4.00	$1.00	

See pages 12 & 13 for important information about properly valuing your donated items.

Electric Appliances, Small

Description	High* Good Condition	Average* Fair Condition	Low* Poor Condition	Total
Toaster Oven				
Name Brand	___$34.00	___$24.00	___$5.00	_____
Other	___$15.00	___$10.00	___$2.00	_____
Vacuum				
Canister				
Name Brand	___$57.00	___$33.00	___$9.00	_____
Other	___$16.00	___$11.00	___$2.00	_____
Handheld	___$13.00	___$9.00	___$2.00	_____
Shop Vac	___$30.00	___$15.00	___$10.00	_____
Stickbroom	___$12.00	___$8.00	___$2.00	_____
Sweeper	___$14.00	___$10.00	___$2.00	_____
Upright				
Name Brand	___$113.00	___$79.00	___$17.00	_____
Other	___$29.00	___$20.00	___$4.00	_____
Vaporizer	___$7.00	___$5.00	___$1.00	_____
Waffle Iron				
Name Brand	___$13.00	___$9.00	___$2.00	_____
Other	___$7.00	___$4.00	___$1.00	_____
Water Filter				
Name Brand	___$27.00	___$19.00	___$4.00	_____
Other	___$10.00	___$6.00	___$1.00	_____
TOTAL ELECTRIC APPLIANCES, SMALL				$

See pages 12 & 13 for important information about properly valuing your donated items.

Electronics, Consumer

Description	High* Good Condition	Average* Fair Condition	Low* Poor Condition	Total
Audio-Video Equipment				
Camcorder				
8mm/Hi 8	___$102.00	___$71.00	___$15.00	_____
Digital	___$213.00	___$149.00	___$32.00	_____
VHS/VHS-C	___$90.00	___$63.00	___$14.00	_____
Cassette Decks	___$22.00	___$15.00	___$3.00	_____
CD Player	___$25.00	___$17.00	___$4.00	_____
DVD Player	___$55.00	___$38.00	___$8.00	_____
Mini Stereo System	___$51.00	___$36.00	___$8.00	_____
Mini-Disc Player	___$46.00	___$32.00	___$7.00	_____
MP3 Player	___$22.00	___$16.00	___$3.00	_____
Portable CD Player	___$18.00	___$12.00	___$3.00	_____
Speakers				
Pair	___$27.00	___$19.00	___$4.00	_____
Surround Sound	___$83.00	___$56.00	___$12.00	_____
Standard Television				
13 inch	___$39.00	___$27.00	___$6.00	_____
19 inch	___$52.00	___$36.00	___$8.00	_____
20 inch	___$58.00	___$41.00	___$9.00	_____
25 inch	___$78.00	___$54.00	___$12.00	_____
27 inch	___$84.00	___$48.00	___$13.00	_____
32 inch	___$172.00	___$94.00	___$26.00	_____
36 inch	___$315.00	___$221.00	___$47.00	_____
Stereo Receivers	___$51.00	___$35.00	___$8.00	_____
Tuners	___$25.00	___$18.00	___$4.00	_____
Turntables	___$13.00	___$9.00	___$2.00	_____
VCR				
Beta	___$12.00	___$3.00	___$2.00	_____
VHS	___$33.00	___$23.00	___$5.00	_____
Walkman	___$8.00	___$6.00	___$1.00	_____

See pages 12 & 13 for important information about properly valuing your donated items.

Electronics, Consumer

Description	High* Good Condition	Average* Fair Condition	Low* Poor Condition	Total
Cameras				
35MM	$34.00	$23.00	$5.00	
APS	$13.00	$8.00	$2.00	
Digital Cameras	$42.00	$30.00	$6.00	
Instamatic	$6.00	$4.00	$1.00	
SLR	$51.00	$27.00	$8.00	
Underwater	$47.00	$17.00	$7.00	
Computer Equipment				
Desktop System	$97.00	$64.00	$10.00	
Laptop Computer	$146.00	$102.00	$22.00	
Monitors - CRT				
15 inch	$15.00	$11.00	$2.00	
16 inch	$18.00	$11.00	$2.00	
17 inch	$30.00	$21.00	$4.00	
19 inch	$85.00	$49.00	$10.00	
20 inch	$96.00	$67.00	$12.00	
21 inch	$107.00	$75.00	$13.00	
Monitors - Flat/LCD				
15 inch	$175.00	$122.00	$21.00	
17 inch	$218.00	$98.00	$26.00	
18 inch	$448.00	$313.00	$54.00	
Keyboards				
Standard	$6.00	$4.00	$1.00	
Wireless	$16.00	$11.00	$2.00	
Printers				
Dot Matrix	$10.00	$7.00	$2.00	
Ink Jet - B&W	$12.00	$9.00	$2.00	
Ink Jet - Color	$17.00	$11.00	$3.00	
Laser - B&W	$39.00	$25.00	$6.00	
Laser - Color	$82.00	$57.00	$12.00	
Photo	$43.00	$25.00	$6.00	
PC Speakers	$17.00	$12.00	$2.00	
Scanners	$85.00	$59.00	$10.00	
Software				
Educational	$5.00	$3.00	$1.00	
Other	$10.00	$7.00	$2.00	

See pages 12 & 13 for important information about properly valuing your donated items.

Electronics, Consumer

Description	High* Good Condition	Average* Fair Condition	Low* Poor Condition	Total
Miscellaneous				
Alarm Clock & Radio	____$15.00	____$11.00	____$2.00	_____
Answering Machine				
Cassette	____$27.00	____$13.00	____$4.00	_____
Digital	____$12.00	____$8.00	____$2.00	_____
PDAs	____$40.00	____$28.00	____$6.00	_____
Telephones				
Corded	____$4.00	____$3.00	____$1.00	_____
Cordless	____$9.00	____$6.00	____$1.00	_____
Video Game Equipment				
GameBoy				
GameBoy Color	____$35.00	____$25.00	____$5.00	_____
GameBoy Original	____$18.00	____$13.00	____$3.00	_____
Microsoft Xbox				
System	____$231.00	____$162.00	____$35.00	_____
Nintendo 64				
Controller	____$11.00	____$8.00	____$2.00	_____
System	____$31.00	____$21.00	____$5.00	_____
Nintendo Gamecube				
System	____$212.00	____$149.00	____$32.00	_____
Sega Dreamcast				
Controller	____$7.00	____$5.00	____$1.00	_____
System	____$74.00	____$52.00	____$11.00	_____
Sony PlayStation 2				
Controller	____$18.00	____$9.00	____$3.00	_____
System	____$160.00	____$112.00	____$24.00	_____
Sony Playstation				
Controller	____$5.00	____$3.00	____$1.00	_____
System	____$28.00	____$20.00	____$4.00	_____
TOTAL ELECTRONICS, CONSUMER			$	

See pages 12 & 13 for important information about properly valuing your donated items.

Entertainment

Description	High* Good Condition	Average* Fair Condition	Low* Poor Condition	Total
Book				
Audio Book	$6.00	$4.00	$1.00	
Cookbook	$7.00	$4.00	$1.00	
Encyclopedias				
Set	$42.00	$33.00	$15.00	
Print Book				
Hardback	$6.00	$3.00	$2.00	
Paperback	$3.00	$2.00	$1.00	
Magazine				
Non-Collector Editions	$1.00	$0.75	$0.50	
Movies and Videos				
DVD	$13.00	$9.00	$2.00	
VHS	$8.00	$6.00	$3.00	
Exercise	$7.00	$4.00	$1.00	
Music				
Cassettes	$6.00	$4.00	$1.00	
CDs	$7.00	$4.00	$1.00	
Records				
45s	$4.00	$3.00	$1.00	
Albums	$6.00	$3.00	$1.00	
TOTAL ENTERTAINMENT			$	

See pages 12 & 13 for important information about properly valuing your donated items.

Exercise Equipment

Description	High* Good Condition	Average* Fair Condition	Low* Poor Condition	Total
Abdominal Equipment				
Ab Away	____$66.00	____$46.00	____$10.00	_____
Ab Doer	____$40.00	____$28.00	____$6.00	_____
Ab Dolly	____$26.00	____$18.00	____$4.00	_____
Ab Fit	____$18.00	____$12.00	____$3.00	_____
Ab Flex	____$7.00	____$5.00	____$1.00	_____
Ab Flex Pro Ab	____$15.00	____$10.00	____$2.00	_____
Ab Force	____$9.00	____$6.00	____$1.00	_____
Ab Max	____$7.00	____$5.00	____$1.00	_____
Ab Rocker	____$13.00	____$9.00	____$2.00	_____
Ab Sculptor	____$15.00	____$11.00	____$2.00	_____
Ab Slide	____$8.00	____$6.00	____$1.00	_____
Ab Sonic	____$25.00	____$17.00	____$4.00	_____
Ab Toner	____$16.00	____$11.00	____$2.00	_____
Ab Trainer	____$28.00	____$20.00	____$4.00	_____
Ab Tronic	____$14.00	____$10.00	____$2.00	_____
Ab Twister	____$11.00	____$8.00	____$2.00	_____
E-Z Crunch	____$6.00	____$4.00	____$1.00	_____
Fast Abs	____$22.00	____$15.00	____$3.00	_____
Exercise Machines				
Nordic Track	____$182.00	____$113.00	____$27.00	_____
Ellipticals				
Computerized	____$500.00	____$355.00	____$75.00	_____
Stair Climber				
Computerized	____$463.00	____$318.00	____$69.00	_____
Manual	____$50.00	____$20.00	____$7.00	_____
Stationary Bikes				
Computerized	____$178.00	____$123.00	____$26.00	_____
Manual	____$50.00	____$20.00	____$7.00	_____
Treadmills				
Computerized	____$415.00	____$290.00	____$62.00	_____

See pages 12 & 13 for important information about properly valuing your donated items.

Exercise Equipment

Description	High* Good Condition	Average* Fair Condition	Low* Poor Condition	Total
Home Gyms	___$324.00	___$227.00	___$49.00	_____
Miscellaneous				
Bar Bells with Weights	___$68.00	___$23.00	___$5.00	_____
Hand and Ankle Weights	___$7.00	___$5.00	___$1.00	_____
Exercise Ball	___$18.00	___$13.00	___$3.00	_____
Heart Rate Monitor	___$69.00	___$48.00	___$10.00	_____
Jump Rope	___$7.00	___$5.00	___$1.00	_____
Weight Belt	___$8.00	___$5.00	___$1.00	_____
Weight Bench	___$75.00	___$20.00	___$10.00	_____
TOTAL EXERCISE EQUIPMENT				$

See pages 12 & 13 for important information about properly valuing your donated items.

Furniture

Description	High* Good Condition	Average* Fair Condition	Low* Poor Condition	Total
Bed				
Box Springs	___$24.00	___$14.00	___$5.00	_____
Bunk	___$118.00	___$75.00	___$30.00	_____
Headboard				
Full	___$95.00	___$54.00	___$24.00	_____
King	___$187.00	___$108.00	___$47.00	_____
Queen	___$116.00	___$66.00	___$29.00	_____
Twin	___$87.00	___$60.00	___$22.00	_____
Mattress				
Full	___$70.00	___$45.00	___$15.00	_____
King	___$78.00	___$65.00	___$19.00	_____
Queen	___$60.00	___$45.00	___$15.00	_____
Twin	___$57.00	___$41.00	___$14.00	_____
Rollaway	___$137.00	___$96.00	___$21.00	_____
Bookshelf	___$110.00	___$52.00	___$24.00	_____
Brass Fireplace Tools	___$19.00	___$13.00	___$5.00	_____
Buffet	___$225.00	___$140.00	___$56.00	_____
Chair				
Bean Bag	___$8.00	___$6.00	___$1.00	_____
Folding Lawn	___$9.00	___$6.00	___$1.00	_____
Living Room	___$90.00	___$45.00	___$19.00	_____
Lounge	___$97.00	___$53.00	___$24.00	_____
Office	___$62.00	___$37.00	___$14.00	_____
Recliner	___$95.00	___$56.00	___$24.00	_____
Rocker				
Swivel	___$114.00	___$64.00	___$26.00	_____
Wooden	___$103.00	___$69.00	___$26.00	_____
Secretary	___$39.00	___$20.00	___$10.00	_____
Chest of Drawers	___$123.00	___$64.00	___$31.00	_____
Coat Rack	___$30.00	___$21.00	___$8.00	_____
Curio	___$179.00	___$79.00	___$25.00	_____

See pages 12 & 13 for important information about properly valuing your donated items.

Furniture

Description	High* Good Condition	Average* Fair Condition	Low* Poor Condition	Total
Desk				
Bedroom	___$98.00	___$61.00	___$25.00	_____
Childs	___$65.00	___$45.00	___$16.00	_____
Office Wood	___$201.00	___$81.00	___$36.00	_____
Wicker	___$100.00	___$50.00	___$20.00	_____
Dining Room Set	___$420.00	___$150.00	___$20.00	_____
Dresser				
Regular	___$176.00	$113.00	___$44.00	_____
with Mirror	___$228.00	$160.00	___$57.00	_____
Entertainment Center	___$156.00	___$86.00	___$39.00	_____
Hutch				
Solid Wood	___$390.00	___$268.00	___$97.00	_____
Lamp				
Desk	___$46.00	___$23.00	___$8.00	_____
Floor	___$63.00	___$31.00	___$15.00	_____
Shades	___$8.00	___$5.00	___$2.00	_____
Swag	___$18.00	___$12.00	___$5.00	_____
Table	___$58.00	___$28.00	___$11.00	_____
Magazine Rack	___$34.00	___$24.00	___$7.00	_____
Nightstand	___$75.00	___$49.00	___$19.00	_____
Piano	___$300.00	___$100.00	___$25.00	_____
Sectional	___$316.00	___$140.00	___$15.00	_____
Sewing Machine	___$75.00	___$30.00	___$10.00	_____
Sofa				
3-Piece Set	___$400.00	___$240.00	___$100.00	_____
Love Seat	___$333.00	___$150.00	___$53.00	_____
Regular	___$253.00	___$116.00	___$45.00	_____
with Recliner	___$305.00	___$145.00	___$65.00	_____
with Sleeper	___$224.00	___$166.00	___$50.00	_____

See pages 12 & 13 for important information about properly valuing your donated items.

Furniture

Description	High* Good Condition	Average* Fair Condition	Low* Poor Condition	Total
Stool				
Set of 4	__ $120.00	__ $47.00	__ $23.00	_____
with Vanity	__ $100.00	__ $49.00	__ $5.00	_____
Table				
Card with Chairs	__ $30.00	__ $15.00	__ $8.00	_____
Coffee	__ $111.00	__ $65.00	__ $28.00	_____
Dining	__ $251.00	__ $160.00	__ $63.00	_____
Dining with 4 Chairs	__ $293.00	__ $203.00	__ $73.00	_____
End	__ $108.00	__ $54.00	__ $27.00	_____
Hall with Mirror	__ $128.00	__ $94.00	__ $32.00	_____
Kitchen	__ $90.00	__ $59.00	__ $22.00	_____
Typewriter				
Electric	__ $25.00	__ $16.00	__ $6.00	_____
Manual	__ $15.00	__ $8.00	__ $4.00	_____
TOTAL FURNITURE				$

Try ItsDeductible Software!

- Direct import into TurboTax® Software
- Quick Search for items
- Receipt and report printing
- Tips and Internet links

It even completes IRS Form 8283, automatically!

www.ItsDeductible.com $19.95

See pages 12 & 13 for important information about properly valuing your donated items.

Games

Description	High* Good Condition	Average* Fair Condition	Low* Poor Condition	Total
Board Games	___$11.00	___$7.00	___$2.00	_____
Computer Games				
PC	___$13.00	___$9.00	___$3.00	_____
Macintosh	___$13.00	___$9.00	___$3.00	_____
VideoGames				
Atari	___$7.00	___$4.00	___$1.00	_____
Coleco	___$11.00	___$5.00	___$2.00	_____
Dreamcast	___$10.00	___$7.00	___$2.00	_____
Gameboy2	___$14.00	___$9.00	___$2.00	_____
GameboyAdvance	___$16.00	___$11.00	___$2.00	_____
Gamecube	___$26.00	___$18.00	___$4.00	_____
Intellivision	___$8.00	___$4.00	___$1.00	_____
Nintendo	___$15.00	___$8.00	___$2.00	_____
Playstation	___$21.00	___$11.00	___$3.00	_____
Playstation2	___$25.00	___$15.00	___$4.00	_____
SuperNintendo	___$10.00	___$6.00	___$2.00	_____
XBox	___$27.00	___$19.00	___$4.00	_____
Other	___$7.00	___$4.00	___$1.00	_____
TOTAL GAMES				$

See pages 12 & 13 for important information about properly valuing your donated items.

Garden Tools

Description	High* Good Condition	Average* Fair Condition	Low* Poor Condition	Total
Anvil Lopper	____$18.00	____$10.00	____$3.00	_____
Bug Zapper	____$15.00	____$11.00	____$2.00	_____
Garden Tool Set	____$9.00	____$6.00	____$1.00	_____
Hedge Trimmer				
Electric	____$40.00	____$28.00	____$6.00	_____
Gas	____$105.00	____$70.00	____$16.00	_____
Hoe	____$29.00	____$12.00	____$4.00	_____
Lawn Mower				
Push	____$170.00	____$92.00	____$26.00	_____
Riding	____$395.00	____$206.00	____$59.00	_____
Leaf Blower				
Electric	____$36.00	____$25.00	____$5.00	_____
Gas	____$83.00	____$57.00	____$12.00	_____
Pest Control	____$19.00	____$11.00	____$3.00	_____
Pressure Washer	____$34.00	____$18.00	____$5.00	_____
Pruner Set	____$32.00	____$21.00	____$5.00	_____
Rake	____$12.00	____$8.00	____$2.00	_____
Shears	____$11.00	____$8.00	____$2.00	_____
Shovel	____$9.00	____$6.00	____$1.00	_____
Sprinkler	____$22.00	____$15.00	____$3.00	_____
Tillers	____$215.00	____$122.00	____$32.00	_____
Trimmer	____$33.00	____$23.00	____$5.00	_____
Watering Can	____$13.00	____$9.00	____$2.00	_____
Wheelbarrow	____$16.00	____$11.00	____$3.00	_____
TOTAL GARDEN TOOLS			$	

See pages 12 & 13 for important information about properly valuing your donated items.

Household Miscellaneous

Description	High* Good Condition	Average* Fair Condition	Low* Poor Condition	Total
Bathroom				
Bathroom Scale	_____$7.00	_____$5.00	_____$2.00	_____
Shower Curtain	_____$13.00	_____$6.00	_____$3.00	_____
Toilet				
Cover	_____$4.00	_____$2.00	_____$1.00	_____
Floor Mat	_____$5.00	_____$4.00	_____$1.00	_____
Tank Cover	_____$5.00	_____$3.00	_____$1.00	_____
Kitchen				
Coffee Mug	_____$2.00	_____$1.00	_____$0.50	_____
Cutting Board (Wooden)	_____$5.00	_____$4.00	_____$1.00	_____
Glassware Tumbler	_____$3.00	_____$1.00	_____$0.50	_____
Hot Pad	_____$2.00	_____$1.00	_____$0.50	_____
Pots and Pans				
Name Brand	_____$35.00	_____$24.00	_____$5.00	_____
Other	_____$23.00	_____$16.00	_____$3.00	_____
Plates				
Name Brand	_____$26.00	_____$16.00	_____$6.00	_____
Other	_____$6.00	_____$2.00	_____$1.00	_____
Shakers - Salt/Pepper	_____$8.00	_____$4.00	_____$2.00	_____
Teapot	_____$10.00	_____$6.00	_____$2.00	_____
Tupperware/Plastic Bowls	_____$6.00	_____$3.00	_____$1.00	_____
Luggage				
Backpack	_____$15.00	_____$6.00	_____$3.00	_____
Carry-On Bag	_____$26.00	_____$13.00	_____$5.00	_____
Set	_____$40.00	_____$19.00	_____$10.00	_____
Suitcase	_____$30.00	_____$16.00	_____$7.00	_____
Miscellaneous				
Ash Tray	_____$5.00	_____$2.00	_____$1.00	_____
Curtains/Drapes				
Bedroom	_____$24.00	_____$12.00	_____$5.00	_____
Dining Room	_____$35.00	_____$21.00	_____$9.00	_____

*See pages 12 & 13 for important information about properly valuing your donated items.

Household Miscellaneous

Description	High* Good Condition	Average* Fair Condition	Low* Poor Condition	Total
Crutches	____$11.00	____$7.00	____$3.00	_____
Doormat	____$10.00	____$6.00	____$3.00	_____
Eyeglasses	____$13.00	____$7.00	____$3.00	_____
Flower Pot	____$9.00	____$5.00	____$2.00	_____
Flower Vase (Glass)	____$10.00	____$4.00	____$2.00	_____
Glass Candles	____$6.00	____$5.00	____$2.00	_____
Heating Pad	____$9.00	____$6.00	____$1.00	_____
Ironing Board	____$7.00	____$5.00	____$2.00	_____
Mini Blinds	____$4.00	____$3.00	____$1.00	_____
Patterns	____$1.50	____$1.00	____$0.50	_____
Picture Frame	____$14.00	____$8.00	____$3.00	_____
Straw Baskets	____$12.00	____$6.00	____$3.00	_____
TOTAL HOUSEHOLD MISCELLANEOUS			$	

See pages 12 & 13 for important information about properly valuing your donated items.

Jewelry

Description	High* Good Condition	Average* Fair Condition	Low* Poor Condition	Total
Watches				
Name Brand	$59.00	$40.00	$9.00	
Other	$9.00	$6.00	$1.00	
Women's Jewelry				
Bracelets				
Charm	$9.00	$6.00	$1.00	
Diamond	$182.00	$63.00	$27.00	
Gold	$44.00	$16.00	$7.00	
Silver	$17.00	$9.00	$3.00	
Brooches				
Crystal	$7.00	$4.00	$1.00	
Diamond	$85.00	$28.00	$13.00	
Gold	$30.00	$10.00	$5.00	
Patriotic	$6.00	$4.00	$1.00	
Pearl	$30.00	$12.00	$5.00	
Silver	$12.00	$7.00	$2.00	
Earrings				
Diamond	$121.00	$46.00	$18.00	
Gold	$18.00	$9.00	$3.00	
Other Gemstone	$11.00	$6.00	$2.00	
Other Materials	$10.00	$5.00	$2.00	
Pearl	$15.00	$8.00	$2.00	
Silver	$7.00	$4.00	$1.00	
Necklaces				
Diamond	$83.00	$28.00	$13.00	
Gold	$34.00	$15.00	$5.00	
Other Gemstones	$22.00	$12.00	$3.00	
Pearl	$32.00	$13.00	$5.00	
Silver	$11.00	$6.00	$2.00	
Sunglasses	$24.00	$16.00	$4.00	
TOTAL JEWELRY				$

See pages 12 & 13 for important information about properly valuing your donated items.

Linens

Description	High* Good Condition	Average* Fair Condition	Low* Poor Condition	Total
Afghan	____$14.00	____$7.00	____$4.00	_____
Aprons	____$3.00	____$2.00	____$1.00	_____
Bath Towels	____$3.00	____$2.00	____$1.00	_____
Bedspread	____$47.00	____$29.00	____$12.00	_____
Blanket				
Heating	____$10.00	____$7.00	____$2.00	_____
Regular	____$9.00	____$5.00	____$2.00	_____
Comforter	____$71.00	____$35.00	____$18.00	_____
Dish Towel	____$2.00	____$1.00	____$1.00	_____
Pillow	____$3.00	____$2.00	____$1.00	_____
Pillow Sham	____$6.00	____$4.00	____$1.00	_____
Pillowcase (Set)	____$3.00	____$2.00	____$1.00	_____
Place Mat (Set)	____$8.00	____$5.00	____$2.00	_____
Quilt	____$37.00	____$16.00	____$6.00	_____
Sheets (Set)	____$12.00	____$5.00	____$3.00	_____
Tablecloth	____$11.00	____$6.00	____$3.00	_____
Throw Pillows	____$22.00	____$10.00	____$4.00	_____
Throw Rug	____$36.00	____$15.00	____$6.00	_____
Washcloth	____$1.50	____$1.00	____$0.50	_____
TOTAL LINENS				$

See pages 12 & 13 for important information about properly valuing your donated items.

Pet Supplies

Description	High* Good Condition	Average* Fair Condition	Low* Poor Condition	Total
Aquariums and Supplies				
Air Pump	$27.00	$18.00	$4.00	
Aquarium Sets	$40.00	$26.00	$6.00	
Bio-Balls	$22.00	$12.00	$3.00	
Decoration				
Gravel	$5.00	$3.00	$1.00	
Other	$9.00	$6.00	$1.00	
Filter				
Bed	$43.00	$30.00	$6.00	
Bio-Sponge	$8.00	$6.00	$1.00	
Canister	$65.00	$43.00	$10.00	
Other	$35.00	$24.00	$5.00	
Filter Cartridge	$14.00	$9.00	$2.00	
Fish Bowl	$13.00	$9.00	$2.00	
Fish Food	$9.00	$5.00	$1.00	
Heater				
Dry	$14.00	$10.00	$2.00	
Submersible	$13.00	$9.00	$2.00	
Light and Hood	$29.00	$18.00	$4.00	
Powerhead	$16.00	$11.00	$2.00	
Protein Skimmer	$64.00	$45.00	$10.00	
Tank				
2 gallon	$15.00	$11.00	$2.00	
10 gallon	$17.00	$11.00	$3.00	
15 gallon	$45.00	$29.00	$7.00	
50 gallon	$104.00	$73.00	$16.00	
55 gallon	$100.00	$70.00	$15.00	
60 gallon	$88.00	$61.00	$13.00	
65 gallon	$123.00	$86.00	$18.00	
75 gallon	$95.00	$66.00	$14.00	
Test Kits	$10.00	$7.00	$2.00	
Thermometer	$15.00	$10.00	$2.00	

See pages 12 & 13 for important information about properly valuing your donated items.

Pet Supplies

Description	High* Good Condition	Average* Fair Condition	Low* Poor Condition	Total
Tools				
Cleaning	_____$8.00	_____$5.00	_____$1.00	_____
Bird Supplies				
Bowls, Feeder, Water Receptacle	_____$10.00	_____$7.00	_____$1.00	_____
Cage	_____$47.00	_____$33.00	_____$7.00	_____
Grooming	_____$18.00	_____$13.00	_____$3.00	_____
Leashes, Collars, Leads	_____$10.00	_____$7.00	_____$1.00	_____
Perch	_____$13.00	_____$9.00	_____$2.00	_____
Pet Door	_____$25.00	_____$18.00	_____$4.00	_____
Pet House	_____$9.00	_____$6.00	_____$1.00	_____
Play Gym	_____$60.00	_____$40.00	_____$9.00	_____
Toys	_____$9.00	_____$6.00	_____$1.00	_____
Cat Supplies				
Bed	_____$18.00	_____$12.00	_____$3.00	_____
Bowls, Feeder, Water Receptacle	_____$13.00	_____$9.00	_____$2.00	_____
Carrier	_____$46.00	_____$32.00	_____$7.00	_____
Grooming	_____$10.00	_____$7.00	_____$2.00	_____
Leashes, Collars, Leads	_____$8.00	_____$6.00	_____$1.00	_____
Litter Box	_____$34.00	_____$23.00	_____$5.00	_____
Litter Box - LitterMaid	_____$65.00	_____$45.00	_____$10.00	_____
Perch	_____$25.00	_____$18.00	_____$4.00	_____
Pet Door	_____$18.00	_____$13.00	_____$3.00	_____
Pet House	_____$36.00	_____$22.00	_____$5.00	_____
Toys	_____$9.00	_____$7.00	_____$1.00	_____
Dog Supplies				
Bed	_____$18.00	_____$13.00	_____$3.00	_____
Bowls, Feeder, Water Receptacle	_____$10.00	_____$7.00	_____$1.00	_____
Kennel	_____$50.00	_____$35.00	_____$8.00	_____
Grooming	_____$15.00	_____$10.00	_____$2.00	_____

See pages 12 & 13 for important information about properly valuing your donated items.

Pet Supplies

Description	High* Good Condition	Average* Fair Condition	Low* Poor Condition	Total
Leashes, Collars, Leads	___ $15.00	___ $9.00	___ $2.00	___
No Bark Collar	___ $51.00	___ $36.00	___ $8.00	___
Pet Door				
Small	___ $13.00	___ $9.00	___ $2.00	___
Medium	___ $32.00	___ $22.00	___ $5.00	___
Large	___ $50.00	___ $35.00	___ $8.00	___
Pet House	___ $19.00	___ $14.00	___ $3.00	___
Toys	___ $9.00	___ $6.00	___ $1.00	___
Rodent Supplies				
Cage	___ $23.00	___ $16.00	___ $3.00	___
Fun Tunnel	___ $10.00	___ $8.00	___ $2.00	___
Pet House	___ $13.00	___ $9.00	___ $2.00	___
TOTAL PET SUPPLIES				$

See pages 12 & 13 for important information about properly valuing your donated items.

Sporting Goods

Description	High* Good Condition	Average* Fair Condition	Low* Poor Condition	Total
Baseball/Softball Equipment				
Baseball	$2.00	$1.00	$1.00	
Bases	$14.00	$4.00	$1.00	
Bat				
Aluminum	$23.00	$8.00	$2.00	
Wood	$10.00	$5.00	$2.00	
Bat Bag	$12.00	$5.00	$1.00	
Batters Helmet	$10.00	$5.00	$1.00	
Catchers				
Chest Protector	$28.00	$10.00	$2.00	
Mask	$24.00	$10.00	$2.00	
Shin Guards	$20.00	$6.00	$2.00	
Glove				
Catchers	$40.00	$22.00	$6.00	
Fielders	$50.00	$35.00	$8.00	
Pants	$10.00	$5.00	$2.00	
Pitchback	$15.00	$10.00	$8.00	
Shoes	$15.00	$6.00	$3.00	
Softball	$4.00	$1.00	$1.00	
Stirrup Socks	$7.00	$3.00	$1.00	
Umpires Chest Protector	$29.00	$10.00	$3.00	
Basketball Equipment				
Basketball	$8.00	$4.00	$1.00	
Biking Equipment				
Mountain Bike				
Name Brand	$210.00	$147.00	$32.00	
Other	$95.00	$67.00	$14.00	
Bike	$80.00	$23.00	$10.00	
Car Rack	$47.00	$25.00	$7.00	
Helmet	$20.00	$13.00	$3.00	

See pages 12 & 13 for important information about properly valuing your donated items.

ItsDeductible™
Turning Donations Into Dollars

Sporting Goods

Description	High* Good Condition	Average* Fair Condition	Low* Poor Condition	Total
Billiards Equipment				
Cue Stick				
Name Brand	_____$36.00	_____$22.00	_____$5.00	_____
Other	_____$9.00	_____$5.00	_____$1.00	_____
Pool Balls	_____$68.00	_____$27.00	_____$10.00	_____
Bowling Equipment				
Bag	_____$14.00	_____$5.00	_____$1.00	_____
Bowling Ball				
Name Brand	_____$45.00	_____$31.00	_____$7.00	_____
Other	_____$12.00	_____$8.00	_____$2.00	_____
Shoes	_____$10.00	_____$5.00	_____$3.00	_____
Boxing Equipment				
Boxing Gloves				
Adult	_____$14.00	_____$10.00	_____$2.00	_____
Child	_____$6.00	_____$4.00	_____$1.00	_____
Coaching Gloves	_____$11.00	_____$7.00	_____$2.00	_____
Jump Rope	_____$11.00	_____$8.00	_____$2.00	_____
Protective Gear				
Head Gear	_____$8.00	_____$5.00	_____$1.00	_____
Punching Bag	_____$21.00	_____$15.00	_____$3.00	_____
Speed Bag	_____$15.00	_____$11.00	_____$2.00	_____
Football Equipment				
Football	_____$9.00	_____$5.00	_____$1.00	_____
Helmet	_____$23.00	_____$16.00	_____$3.00	_____
Pad				
Neck	_____$8.00	_____$4.00	_____$1.00	_____
Thigh	_____$9.00	_____$6.00	_____$1.00	_____
Shoulder	_____$23.00	_____$13.00	_____$3.00	_____
Shoes	_____$11.00	_____$8.00	_____$2.00	_____

See pages 12 & 13 for important information about properly valuing your donated items.

Sporting Goods

Description	High* Good Condition	Average* Fair Condition	Low* Poor Condition	Total
Golfing Equipment				
Bag				
Name Brand	___$64.00	___$37.00	___$10.00	_____
Other	___$23.00	___$16.00	___$4.00	_____
Ball	___$2.00	___$1.00	___$0.50	_____
Head Covers	___$13.00	___$9.00	___$2.00	_____
Clubs				
8-Piece Set	___$139.00	___$98.00	___$21.00	_____
Iron	___$26.00	___$17.00	___$4.00	_____
Putter	___$33.00	___$23.00	___$5.00	_____
Driver/Wood	___$55.00	___$39.00	___$8.00	_____
Wedge	___$19.00	___$14.00	___$3.00	_____
Shoes				
Name Brand	___$27.00	___$17.00	___$4.00	_____
Other	___$16.00	___$11.00	___$2.00	_____
Hockey Equipment				
Gloves	___$29.00	___$16.00	___$4.00	_____
Goal	___$37.00	___$26.00	___$6.00	_____
Helmet				
Goalie	___$72.00	___$39.00	___$11.00	_____
Player	___$22.00	___$16.00	___$3.00	_____
Pads				
Goalie	___$65.00	___$10.00	___$3.00	_____
Shoulder	___$34.00	___$9.00	___$3.00	_____
Pants	___$21.00	___$13.00	___$3.00	_____
Stick	___$51.00	___$30.00	___$8.00	_____
Skating Equipment				
Hockey Skates				
Name Brand	___$72.00	___$50.00	___$11.00	_____
Other	___$8.00	___$5.00	___$1.00	_____
Ice Skates, Adult				
Name Brand	___$19.00	___$10.00	___$3.00	_____
Other	___$9.00	___$6.00	___$1.00	_____

See pages 12 & 13 for important information about properly valuing your donated items.

Sporting Goods

Description	High* Good Condition	Average* Fair Condition	Low* Poor Condition	Total
Ice Skates, Child				
Name Brand	$20.00	$14.00	$3.00	
Other	$6.00	$4.00	$1.00	
In-Line Skates				
Name Brand	$59.00	$41.00	$9.00	
Other	$22.00	$15.00	$3.00	
Roller Skates				
Name Brand	$33.00	$15.00	$5.00	
Other	$14.00	$5.00	$2.00	
Skateboard				
Name Brand	$61.00	$42.00	$9.00	
Other	$15.00	$11.00	$2.00	
Ski Equipment				
Snow Skiing				
Snowboard	$49.00	$12.00	$3.00	
Ski Boot Carrier	$35.00	$9.00	$1.00	
Ski Boots - Adult	$35.00	$11.00	$4.00	
Ski Boots - Child	$20.00	$10.00	$3.00	
Ski Glider	$36.00	$10.00	$7.00	
Ski Goggles	$19.00	$9.00	$3.00	
Ski Poles	$14.00	$5.00	$2.00	
Skis (Pair)	$65.00	$13.00	$7.00	
Water Skiing				
Knee Board	$30.00	$12.00	$7.00	
Water Pair	$50.00	$20.00	$7.00	
Water Slalom	$30.00	$14.00	$8.00	
Soccer Equipment				
Bag	$13.00	$8.00	$2.00	
Ball	$9.00	$6.00	$1.00	
Cleats				
Name Brand	$21.00	$13.00	$3.00	
Other	$10.00	$7.00	$1.00	
Goalie Gloves	$13.00	$9.00	$2.00	

See pages 12 & 13 for important information about properly valuing your donated items.

Sporting Goods

Description	High* Good Condition	Average* Fair Condition	Low* Poor Condition	Total
Jerseys	____$13.00	____$9.00	____$2.00	_____
Shin Guards	____$4.00	____$3.00	____$1.00	_____
Shorts	____$7.00	____$5.00	____$1.00	_____
Socks	____$6.00	____$4.00	____$1.00	_____
Tennis Equipment				
Tennis Racket				
Name Brand	____$58.00	____$40.00	____$9.00	_____
Other	____$20.00	____$14.00	____$3.00	_____
TOTAL SPORTING GOODS			$	

Try ItsDeductible Software!

- Direct import into TurboTax® Software
- Quick Search for items
- Receipt and report printing
- Tips and Internet links

It even completes IRS Form 8283, automatically!

www.ItsDeductible.com $19.95

See pages 12 & 13 for important information about properly valuing your donated items.

Tools

Description	High* Good Condition	Average* Fair Condition	Low* Poor Condition	Total
Adjustable Wrench	$11.00	$7.00	$2.00	
Air Hose	$10.00	$7.00	$1.00	
Bench Vises	$14.00	$10.00	$2.00	
Brad Nailer	$44.00	$31.00	$7.00	
Chainsaws	$152.00	$106.00	$23.00	
Chisel	$10.00	$5.00	$2.00	
Clamp	$16.00	$11.00	$2.00	
Crown Stapler	$46.00	$32.00	$7.00	
Electric Drill	$62.00	$44.00	$9.00	
Flashlight	$4.00	$2.00	$1.00	
Grinder	$23.00	$16.00	$3.00	
Hammer	$10.00	$7.00	$2.00	
Heat Gun Kit	$27.00	$19.00	$4.00	
Impact Wrench	$44.00	$30.00	$7.00	
Level	$27.00	$14.00	$4.00	
Level - Laser with Stud Finder	$35.00	$23.00	$5.00	
Ratchet	$23.00	$11.00	$4.00	
Router	$32.00	$23.00	$5.00	
Router Bits	$12.00	$8.00	$2.00	
Sander				
Belt	$35.00	$24.00	$5.00	
Finishing	$21.00	$15.00	$3.00	
Orbital	$28.00	$19.00	$4.00	
Saw				
Circular	$29.00	$20.00	$4.00	
Hand	$13.00	$8.00	$2.00	

See pages 12 & 13 for important information about properly valuing your donated items.

Tools

Description	High* Good Condition	Average* Fair Condition	Low* Poor Condition	Total
Screwdriver				
Cordless	____$25.00	____$9.00	____$4.00	_____
Drywall	____$45.00	____$31.00	____$7.00	_____
Tape Measure	____$8.00	____$6.00	____$1.00	_____
Tool Carriers	____$17.00	____$10.00	____$3.00	_____
Utility Knife	____$11.00	____$7.00	____$2.00	_____
Wire Cutters	____$7.00	____$5.00	____$1.00	_____
Other Small Hand Tools	____$4.00	____$2.00	____$1.00	_____
TOTAL TOOLS			$	

See pages 12 & 13 for important information about properly valuing your donated items.

Toys

Description	High* Good Condition	Average* Fair Condition	Low* Poor Condition	Total
Bionicles	_____$3.00	_____$2.00	_____$1.00	_____
Disney Figures	_____$3.00	_____$2.00	_____$1.00	_____
Electronic Pet	_____$9.00	_____$6.00	_____$1.00	_____
Fisher Price				
Briarberry	_____$6.00	_____$4.00	_____$1.00	_____
Dollhouse	_____$7.00	_____$5.00	_____$1.00	_____
Great Adventures	_____$7.00	_____$5.00	_____$1.00	_____
Little People	_____$3.00	_____$2.00	_____$1.00	_____
Rescue Heroes	_____$6.00	_____$4.00	_____$1.00	_____
Furby	_____$7.00	_____$5.00	_____$1.00	_____
G.I. Joe	_____$8.00	_____$5.00	_____$1.00	_____
Harry Potter	_____$2.00	_____$1.00	_____$0.50	_____
Hot Wheels	_____$2.00	_____$1.00	_____$0.50	_____
Little Tikes				
Cars & Trucks	_____$8.00	_____$5.00	_____$1.00	_____
Climbers	_____$50.00	_____$35.00	_____$7.00	_____
Dollhouse	_____$3.00	_____$2.00	_____$1.00	_____
Furniture	_____$20.00	_____$14.00	_____$3.00	_____
Infant	_____$6.00	_____$4.00	_____$1.00	_____
Outdoor & Seasonal Play	_____$10.00	_____$7.00	_____$1.00	_____
Ride-Ons	_____$9.00	_____$6.00	_____$1.00	_____
Roleplay	_____$7.00	_____$5.00	_____$1.00	_____
Toddler-Preschool	_____$7.00	_____$5.00	_____$1.00	_____
Masters of the Universe Figures	_____$6.00	_____$4.00	_____$1.00	_____
Matchbox Car	_____$2.50	_____$1.00	_____$0.50	_____
Miscellaneous				
Large Toys	_____$15.00	_____$10.00	_____$5.00	_____
Small Toys	_____$3.00	_____$2.00	_____$1.00	_____
Puzzles	_____$4.00	_____$2.00	_____$1.00	_____

*See pages 12 & 13 for important information about properly valuing your donated items.

Toys

Description	High* Good Condition	Average* Fair Condition	Low* Poor Condition	Total
Scooter - Folding	____$16.00	____$11.00	____$2.00	____
Star Wars Figures	____$5.00	____$3.00	____$1.00	
Stuffed Animal				
Large	____$12.00	____$6.00	____$4.00	____
Small	____$7.00	____$4.00	____$2.00	____
Transformers	____$5.00	____$3.00	____$1.00	____
Ty Attic Treasures	____$11.00	____$7.00	____$2.00	____
TOTAL TOYS				$

Try ItsDeductible Software!

- Direct import into TurboTax® Software
- Quick Search for items
- Receipt and report printing
- Tips and Internet links

It even completes IRS Form 8283, automatically!

www.ItsDeductible.com $19.95

*See pages 12 & 13 for important information about properly valuing your donated items.

Section 7 Valuation Worksheets

Donations can take many different forms. For example, if you perform volunteer work for a charity or church and spend your own money or use your own vehicle, you can deduct your actual expenses. The following worksheets will help you track the following donations:

- Custom Items – use this form for items you do not find in the workbook.
- Property Donations – track donations of stocks, bonds and mutual funds
- Mileage Expense – record the use of your personal automobile for a charity
- Monetary Donations – gifts by cash, credit card or check can be recorded here
- Out-of-Pocket Expenses – use this form for miscellaneous expenses for charitable work, including supplies purchased for your classroom.

Custom Item Donations

ItsDeductible contains thousands of item values for the most commonly donated items. However, you may be donating items that are not included in ItsDeductible.

The following form allows you to track all of your **custom item donations**.

When creating a custom item donation, you will be responsible for determining the value of the item. Common methods you might use:

- Determine the value of comparable items at a <u>thrift or consignment shop</u>.
- Have an <u>appraisal</u> done on your item. You will typically only want to do this for expensive items like jewelry or art.
- Use a <u>catalog</u> for collectible items such as stamps, coins or baseball cards.
- Utilize <u>comparable sales</u> for things like real estate or other valuable assets.
- Visit StrongNumbers.com or Ebay.com for unique household items.

For items valued over $500, try to include the original purchase date and value for your records.

Custom Item Donations

Item Description	
Condition	❏ Good ❏ Fair ❏ Poor
Quantity	
Value $	
Method of Valuation	

Complete the following only if the Item Value is greater than $500

Date Acquired	
Cost or Adjusted Basis	
How was this Item Acquired?	

Item Description	
Condition	❏ Good ❏ Fair ❏ Poor
Quantity	
Value $	
Method of Valuation	

Complete the following only if the Item Value is greater than $500

Date Acquired	
Cost or Adjusted Basis	
How was this Item Acquired?	

Custom Item Donations

Item Description	
Condition	☐ Good ☐ Fair ☐ Poor
Quantity	
Value $	
Method of Valuation	

Complete the following only if the Item Value is greater than $500

Date Acquired	
Cost or Adjusted Basis	
How was this Item Acquired?	

Item Description	
Condition	☐ Good ☐ Fair ☐ Poor
Quantity	
Value $	
Method of Valuation	

Complete the following only if the Item Value is greater than $500

Date Acquired	
Cost or Adjusted Basis	
How was this Item Acquired?	

Custom Item Donations

Item Description	
Condition	❏ **Good** ❏ **Fair** ❏ **Poor**
Quantity	
Value $	
Method of Valuation	
Complete the following only if the Item Value is greater than $500	
Date Acquired	
Cost or Adjusted Basis	
How was this Item Acquired?	

Item Description	
Condition	❏ **Good** ❏ **Fair** ❏ **Poor**
Quantity	
Value $	
Method of Valuation	
Complete the following only if the Item Value is greater than $500	
Date Acquired	
Cost or Adjusted Basis	
How was this Item Acquired?	

ItsDeductible™
Turning Donations Into Dollars

Custom Item Donations

Item Description	
Condition	☐ Good ☐ Fair ☐ Poor
Quantity	
Value $	
Method of Valuation	
Complete the following only if the Item Value is greater than $500	
Date Acquired	
Cost or Adjusted Basis	
How was this Item Acquired?	

Item Description	
Condition	☐ Good ☐ Fair ☐ Poor
Quantity	
Value $	
Method of Valuation	
Complete the following only if the Item Value is greater than $500	
Date Acquired	
Cost or Adjusted Basis	
How was this Item Acquired?	

Custom Item Donations

Item Description	
Condition	☐ **Good** ☐ **Fair** ☐ **Poor**
Quantity	
Value $	
Method of Valuation	

Complete the following only if the Item Value is greater than $500

Date Acquired	
Cost or Adjusted Basis	
How was this Item Acquired?	

Item Description	
Condition	☐ **Good** ☐ **Fair** ☐ **Poor**
Quantity	
Value $	
Method of Valuation	

Complete the following only if the Item Value is greater than $500

Date Acquired	
Cost or Adjusted Basis	
How was this Item Acquired?	

Total Custom Item Donations

ItsDeductible™
Turning Donations Into Dollars

Property Donations Tracking

A property donation is defined as a donation of stocks, bonds, or mutual funds to a qualified organization. Property Donations may be subject to limitations based on your Adjusted Gross Income. Contact your Tax Professional to see if your donation is subject to these limitations.

Donated To	**Date** _____
Item Description	**Symbol/Ticker** _____
Property Type	❑ **Stock** ❑ **Bond** ❑ **Mutual Fund**
Date Acquired	
Cost or Adjusted Basis	
Fair-Market-Value on Date of Donation*	

Donated To	**Date** _____
Item Description	**Symbol/Ticker** _____
Property Type	❑ **Stock** ❑ **Bond** ❑ **Mutual Fund**
Date Acquired	
Cost or Adjusted Basis	
Fair-Market-Value on Date of Donation*	

* Determine the Fair-Market-Value of your property donation by visiting this ItsDeductible website: **http://www.ItsDeductible.com/prodsupport/propertyvalue.html**

Property Donations Tracking

Donated To	**Date** _____
Item Description	**Symbol/Ticker** _____
Property Type	☐ **Stock** ☐ **Bond** ☐ **Mutual Fund**
Date Acquired	
Cost or Adjusted Basis	
Fair-Market-Value on Date of Donation*	

Donated To	**Date** _____
Item Description	**Symbol/Ticker** _____
Property Type	☐ **Stock** ☐ **Bond** ☐ **Mutual Fund**
Date Acquired	
Cost or Adjusted Basis	
Fair-Market-Value on Date of Donation*	

Donated To	**Date** _____
Item Description	**Symbol/Ticker** _____
Property Type	☐ **Stock** ☐ **Bond** ☐ **Mutual Fund**
Date Acquired	
Cost or Adjusted Basis	
Fair-Market-Value on Date of Donation*	

Total Property Donations	

Mileage Expense Tracking

Travel costs are deductible when they are not reimbursed by the charity. The current IRS mileage deduction is 14 cents per mile. Toll and parking fees can be deducted in addition to the 14-cent mileage deduction.

Description	Date	Miles Driven	Per Mile	Extended Total
Vacation Bible School			$.14	$
Coaching Youth Sports			$.14	$
Food Bank			$.14	$
			$.14	$
			$.14	$
			$.14	$
			$.14	$
			$.14	$
			$.14	$
			$.14	$
			$.14	$
			$.14	$
			$.14	$
			$.14	$
			$.14	$
			$.14	$
			$.14	$
			$.14	$
			$.14	$

Mileage Expense Tracking

Description	Date	Miles Driven	Per Mile	Extended Total
			$.14	$
			$.14	$
			$.14	$
			$.14	$
			$.14	$
			$.14	$
			$.14	$
			$.14	$
			$.14	$
			$.14	$
			$.14	$
			$.14	$
			$.14	$
			$.14	$
			$.14	$
			$.14	$
			$.14	$
			$.14	$
Mileage Expenses Total				

ItsDeductible™
Turning Donations Into Dollars

Monetary Donation Tracking

Monetary Donations are donations made to a charitable organization in the form of cash, check, credit card or debit card.

Description	Date	Check or Credit Card Number	Receipt?	Amount
American Cancer Society			☐ Yes ☐ No	$
United Way			☐ Yes ☐ No	$
Boy Scouts of America			☐ Yes ☐ No	$
Red Cross			☐ Yes ☐ No	$
			☐ Yes ☐ No	$
			☐ Yes ☐ No	$
			☐ Yes ☐ No	$
			☐ Yes ☐ No	$
			☐ Yes ☐ No	$
			☐ Yes ☐ No	$
			☐ Yes ☐ No	$
			☐ Yes ☐ No	$
			☐ Yes ☐ No	$
			☐ Yes ☐ No	$

Monetary Donation Tracking

Description	Date	Check or Credit Card Number	Receipt?	Amount
			☐ Yes ☐ No	$
			☐ Yes ☐ No	$
			☐ Yes ☐ No	$
			☐ Yes ☐ No	$
			☐ Yes ☐ No	$
			☐ Yes ☐ No	$
			☐ Yes ☐ No	$
			☐ Yes ☐ No	$
			☐ Yes ☐ No	$
			☐ Yes ☐ No	$
			☐ Yes ☐ No	$
			☐ Yes ☐ No	$
			☐ Yes ☐ No	$
			☐ Yes ☐ No	$
			☐ Yes ☐ No	$

Monetary Donation Tracking

Description	Date	Check or Credit Card Number	Receipt?	Amount
			☐ Yes ☐ No	$
			☐ Yes ☐ No	$
			☐ Yes ☐ No	$
			☐ Yes ☐ No	$
			☐ Yes ☐ No	$
			☐ Yes ☐ No	$
			☐ Yes ☐ No	$
			☐ Yes ☐ No	$
			☐ Yes ☐ No	$
			☐ Yes ☐ No	$
			☐ Yes ☐ No	$
			☐ Yes ☐ No	$
			☐ Yes ☐ No	$
			☐ Yes ☐ No	$
			☐ Yes ☐ No	$

Monetary Donation Tracking

Description	Date	Check or Credit Card Number	Receipt?	Amount
			☐ Yes ☐ No	$
			☐ Yes ☐ No	$
			☐ Yes ☐ No	$
			☐ Yes ☐ No	$
			☐ Yes ☐ No	$
			☐ Yes ☐ No	$
			☐ Yes ☐ No	$
			☐ Yes ☐ No	$
			☐ Yes ☐ No	$
			☐ Yes ☐ No	$
			☐ Yes ☐ No	$
			☐ Yes ☐ No	$
			☐ Yes ☐ No	$
			☐ Yes ☐ No	$
Total Monetary Donations				$

Out-of-Pocket Expense Tracking

Out-of-pocket expenses are defined as those expenses incurred while performing volunteer charitable work, or as a function of participation in or with a tax-exempt organization.

Description	Date	Check or Credit Card Number	Receipt?	Amount
Church Youth Group Pizza Party			☐ Yes ☐ No	$
Donuts for Boy Scouts of America			☐ Yes ☐ No	$
Food purchase for the Food Bank			☐ Yes ☐ No	$
			☐ Yes ☐ No	$
			☐ Yes ☐ No	$
			☐ Yes ☐ No	$
			☐ Yes ☐ No	$
			☐ Yes ☐ No	$
			☐ Yes ☐ No	$
			☐ Yes ☐ No	$
			☐ Yes ☐ No	$
			☐ Yes ☐ No	$
			☐ Yes ☐ No	$
			☐ Yes ☐ No	$

Out-of-Pocket Expense Tracking

Description	Date	Check or Credit Card Number	Receipt?	Amount
			☐ Yes ☐ No	$
			☐ Yes ☐ No	$
			☐ Yes ☐ No	$
			☐ Yes ☐ No	$
			☐ Yes ☐ No	$
			☐ Yes ☐ No	$
			☐ Yes ☐ No	$
			☐ Yes ☐ No	$
			☐ Yes ☐ No	$
			☐ Yes ☐ No	$
			☐ Yes ☐ No	$
			☐ Yes ☐ No	$
			☐ Yes ☐ No	$
			☐ Yes ☐ No	$
			☐ Yes ☐ No	$

Out-of-Pocket Expense Tracking

Description	Date	Check or Credit Card Number	Receipt?	Amount
			☐ Yes ☐ No	$
			☐ Yes ☐ No	$
			☐ Yes ☐ No	$
			☐ Yes ☐ No	$
			☐ Yes ☐ No	$
			☐ Yes ☐ No	$
			☐ Yes ☐ No	$
			☐ Yes ☐ No	$
			☐ Yes ☐ No	$
			☐ Yes ☐ No	$
			☐ Yes ☐ No	$
			☐ Yes ☐ No	$
			☐ Yes ☐ No	$
			☐ Yes ☐ No	$
			☐ Yes ☐ No	$

Out-of-Pocket Expense Tracking

Description	Date	Check or Credit Card Number	Receipt?	Amount
			☐ Yes ☐ No	$
			☐ Yes ☐ No	$
			☐ Yes ☐ No	$
			☐ Yes ☐ No	$
			☐ Yes ☐ No	$
			☐ Yes ☐ No	$
			☐ Yes ☐ No	$
			☐ Yes ☐ No	$
			☐ Yes ☐ No	$
			☐ Yes ☐ No	$
			☐ Yes ☐ No	$
			☐ Yes ☐ No	$
			☐ Yes ☐ No	$
			☐ Yes ☐ No	$
Total Out-of-Pocket Donations			$	

Charitable Organizations Information

Complete the information below for each charity to which you donate. This will be useful during your income tax preparation.

Name of Charity				
Address				
Donation Dates				
Donation Amount				

Name of Charity				
Address				
Donation Dates				
Donation Amount				

Name of Charity				
Address				
Donation Dates				
Donation Amount				

Name of Charity				
Address				
Donation Dates				
Donation Amount				

Charitable Organizations Information

Name of Charity	
Address	
Donation Dates				
Donation Amount				

Name of Charity	
Address	
Donation Dates				
Donation Amount				

Name of Charity	
Address	
Donation Dates				
Donation Amount				

Name of Charity	
Address	
Donation Dates				
Donation Amount				

Charitable Organizations Information

Name of Charity				
Address				
Donation Dates				
Donation Amount				

Name of Charity				
Address				
Donation Dates				
Donation Amount				

Name of Charity				
Address				
Donation Dates				
Donation Amount				

Name of Charity				
Address				
Donation Dates				
Donation Amount				

Charitable Organizations Information

Name of Charity				
Address				
Donation Dates				
Donation Amount				

Name of Charity				
Address				
Donation Dates				
Donation Amount				

Name of Charity				
Address				
Donation Dates				
Donation Amount				

Name of Charity				
Address				
Donation Dates				
Donation Amount				

Tax Preparation Worksheet

To prepare your income taxes, you will need to know the total of your donations. Total all of your donations and record the amounts below.

Donation Date & Charity Name	$
Donation Date & Charity Name	$
Donation Date & Charity Name	$
Donation Date & Charity Name	$
Donation Date & Charity Name	$
Donation Date & Charity Name	$
Donation Date & Charity Name	$
Donation Date & Charity Name	$
Total Item Donations	$
Total Mileage Expenses	$
Total Monetary Donations	$
Total Out-of-Pocket Expenses	$
GRAND TOTAL	$
Estimated Federal and State Tax Rates Combined* (Use 34% if unsure)	%
Approximate Tax Savings	$

* Determine your state tax rate by visiting your state's tax website. You can reach it easily through the ItsDeductible website at: http://www.ItsDeductible.com/html/help_statetax.shtml

Notes

Notes

Notes

Notes

Notes

Notes

Notes

Notes

Notes

Notes

Notes

Notes